Dearest Kirsten

Thank you for

me this year. I could

Beyond the Wave

not have finished this book without you. Your belief in me has allowed me to go on this difficult but amazing journey.

[illegible]

Beyond the Wave

A TSUNAMI SURVIVOR'S STORY

TRISHA BROADBRIDGE

WITH

JON CARNEGIE

First published in 2005

Allen & Unwin Pty Ltd
83 Alexander Street
Crows Nest NSW 2065
Australia
Phone: (61 2) 8425 0100
Fax: (61 2) 9906 2218
Email: info@allenandunwin.com
Web: www.allenandunwin.com

National Library of Australia
Cataloguing-in-publication entry:
Broadbridge, Trisha.
Beyond the wave : a tsunami survivor's story.

ISBN 1 74114 806 5.

1. Broadbridge, Trisha. 2. Broadbridge, Troy. 3. Indian Ocean Tsunami, 2004 – Personal narratives, Australian. 4. Women disaster victims – Thailand – Phi Phi Island - Biography. I. Carnegie, Jon. II. Title.

959.3044

Cover and text design by Phil Campbell
Maps by Guy Holt
Typeset by J&M Typesetting
Printed in Australia by McPherson's Printing Group
10 9 8 7 6 5 4 3 2 1

I want to know if you can get up
after the night of grief and despair,
weary or bruised to the bone,
and do what needs to be done for the children.
It doesn't interest me where or what or with
whom you have studied.
I want to know what sustains you from the
inside when all else falls away.
I want to know if you can be alone with yourself
and if you truly like the company you keep in
empty moments.

From *The Invitation* by Oriah Mountain Dreamer

Contents

TROY BROADBRIDGE

5 October 1980 – 26 December 2004

Troy Broadbridge was tragically killed in the Boxing Day tsunami while on honeymoon in Thailand with his new wife Trisha. Troy came from a football family: his father Wayne played for Port Adelaide in the SANFL. Troy started his career at the Melbourne Football Club (MFC) in 1999 after being recruited from the SANFL, playing in the seconds at Sandringham before being elevated to the senior list in 2001. The young South Australian boy was always destined to play football with his explosive speed and thumping kick. Two shoulder injuries and a knee injury did not deter Troy from his path, and he continued his training to return strongly and have his best year in 2004. Troy was a dual premiership player for Sandringham and played forty games for Melbourne, and he will be remembered for his tenacity and dedication to the sport he loved so much, his courage in overcoming setbacks, and his generosity of spirit with fellow players.

Player Honours
MFC Most Improved Player 2001
Brownlow Medal: 2002 votes – 1; career votes – 1

Player Stats
MFC Rookie Draft Selection 1999 – Guernsey No. 50
Elevated to MFC senior list 2001 – Guernsey No. 20
Made senior debut Round 8 2001 vs Essendon
Role in team: tall defender
Career totals AFL: 40 games, 2 goals

VFL Premierships (Sandringham) – 2000 and 2004
MFC Finals – Elimination Final vs Essendon, 2004

Author's Note

The hardest thing about writing this book has been finding the words to express what happened to me and thousands of others on 26 December 2004. While my story has become a focus for the media, I know there are hundreds out there who have begun the process of putting back together their shattered lives in silence. To me, they are the real heroes of the tsunami: the Thai fisherman who lost his whole family but will wake up this morning and begin to mend his nets; the Australian family forced to sift through the remains of their loved one's luggage; the orphaned girl in Sri Lanka who will study English at school today in the hope it will lead to a better future; and the Acehnese mother who is caring for an orphaned child in place of the one she lost. They are the heroes. They are the people whose actions embody the very best the human spirit has to offer.

This is my story but I dedicate this book to them, and to Troy, my husband and soul mate.

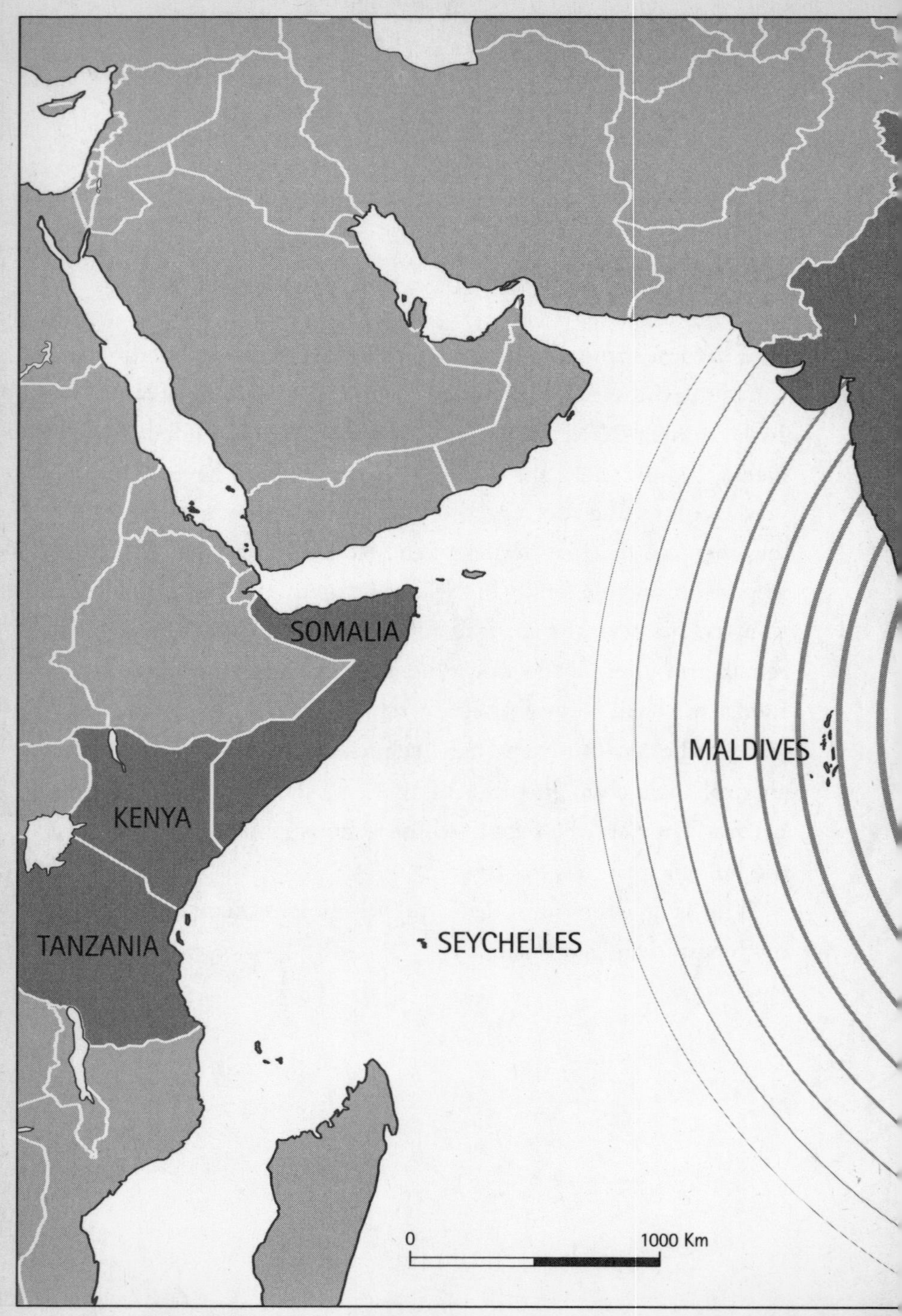

Countries hit by the 2004 Boxing Day tsunami

BANGLADESH
INDIA
MYANMAR
(BURMA)
THAILAND
ANDAMAN AND
NICOBAR ISLANDS
SRI LANKA
MALAYSIA
INDONESIA
AUSTRALIA

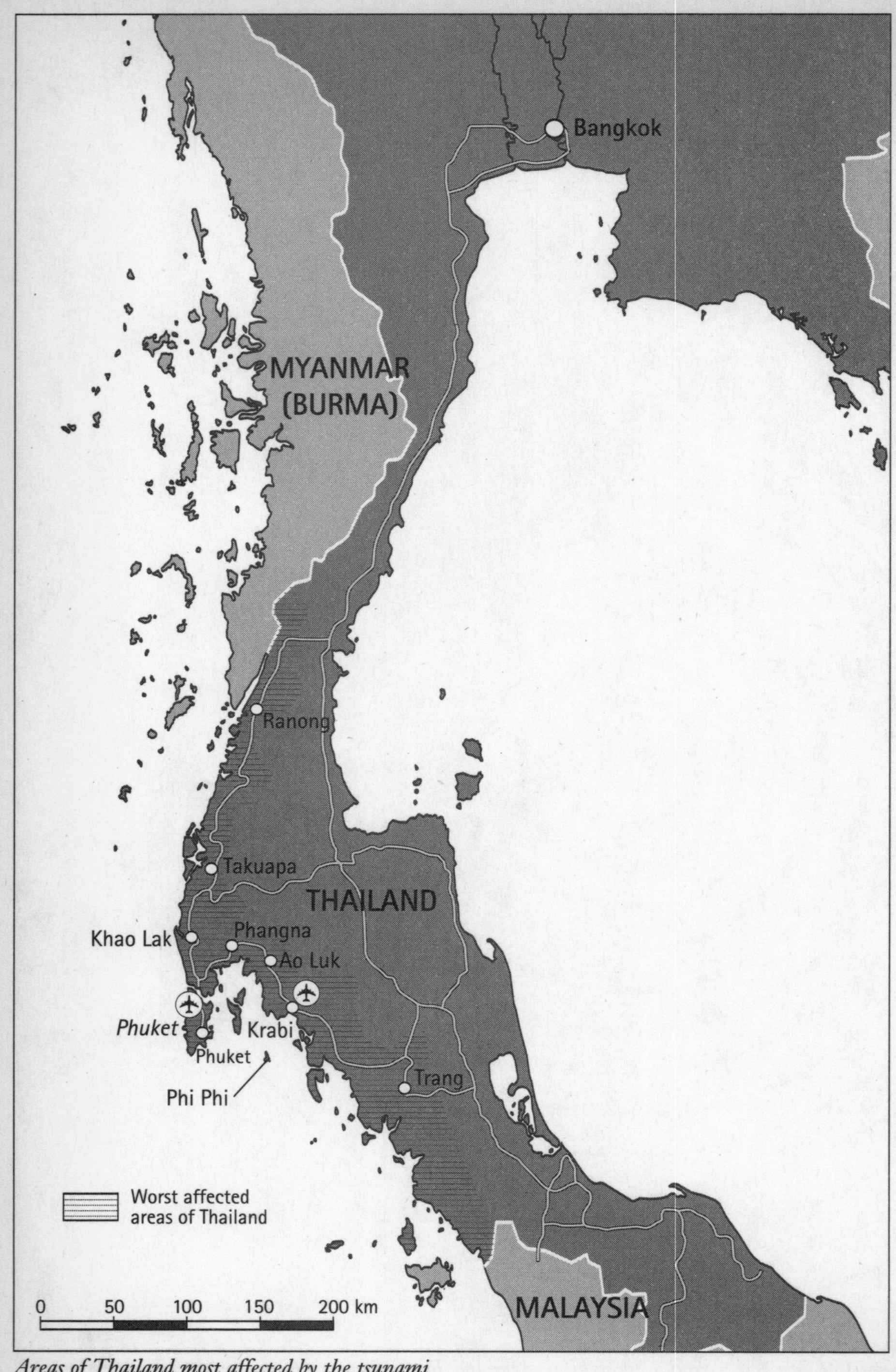

Areas of Thailand most affected by the tsunami

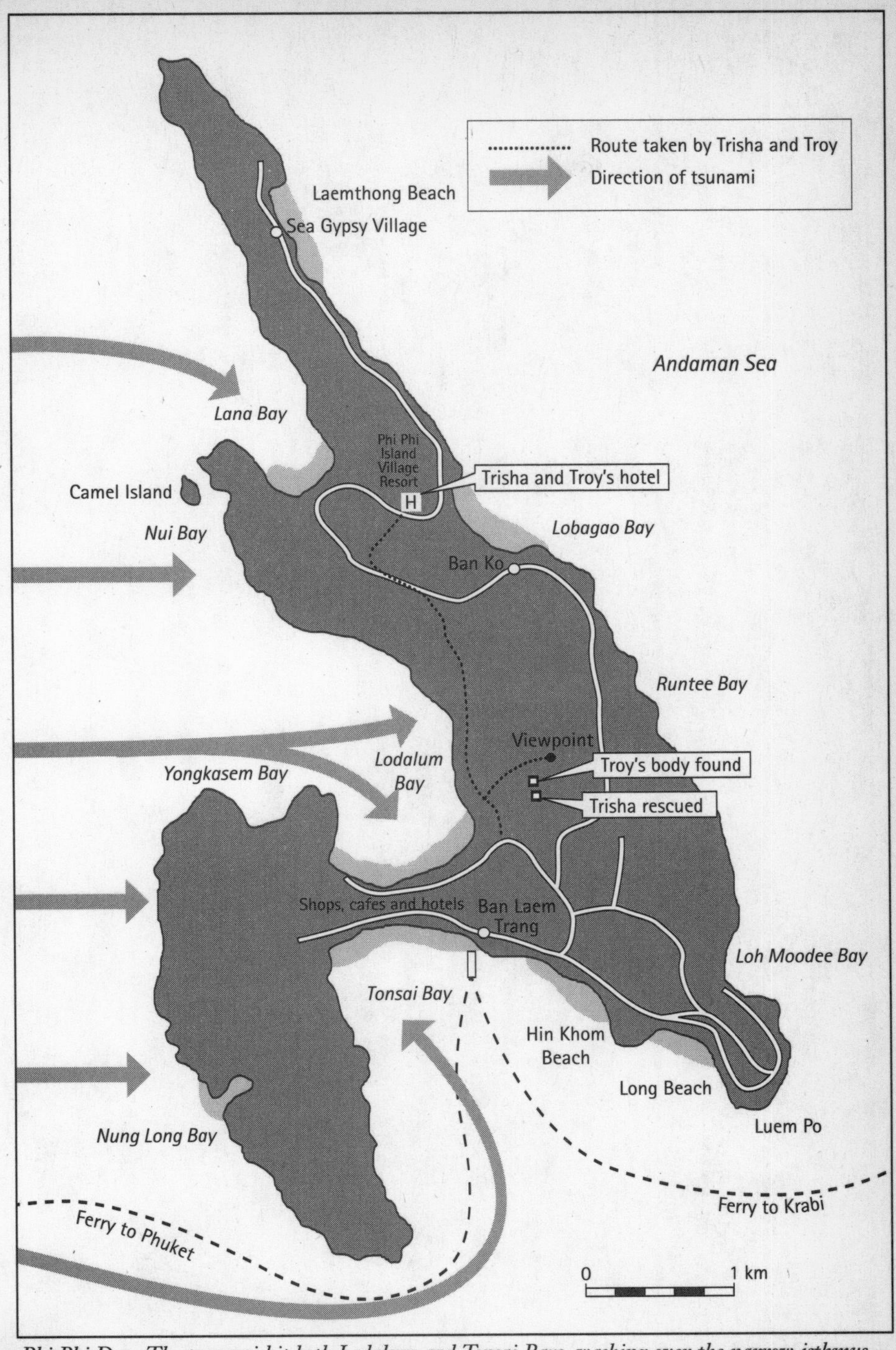

Phi Phi Don. The tsunami hit both Lodalum and Tonsai Bays, washing over the narrow isthmus between the two several times.

ยินดีต้อนรับ
WELCOME & BIENVENUE
TO
PHI PHI DREAM
A SERVICE WITH SMILE

Part One

The Wave

Chapter 1

Boxing Day 2004

On the morning of 26 December 2004, as usual I woke earlier than Troy. I opened my eyes and I was facing the door. Troy's luggage was in the corner, his brown shorts and Billabong singlet lying on the floor, still wet from the day before. I thought how much I loved Troy in that singlet.

Troy was in training, so even though we were on our honeymoon, we hadn't been drinking the night before. While the other guests were getting into it at a Christmas party, we had gone to the resort's 'cinema' – a DVD playing in a room – where they were showing *50 First Dates*. Needless to say we were the only ones there. We had a long talk that night about our plans for a family. We wanted to have children young, and since Troy had just signed a two-year deal at Melbourne Football Club, the following year seemed like the best time. Troy loved kids, and that night he had said he hoped to have twins.

I rolled over and put my arm around him. As he woke he turned in the bed and laid his head on my chest, then moved up and kissed my forehead. 'Good morning, Toots,' he said. Troy called me Toots, Trishy or Skipper. Skipper was my favourite, because it meant captain of the team, and I suppose it was Troy's way of saying that sometimes I was leading him.

'So what should we do today, Skipper?' he asked as we contemplated getting up for a resort-style breakfast. We decided to walk over the mountain which divided our resort from Phi Phi village and go up to the Viewpoint on Tonsai Bay. The previous day we had booked to do this walk with a guide, but the trip was cancelled as no one else booked in. We thought we could try it on our own.

Breakfast at the resort was amazing. We sat on a balcony overlooking the ocean and the little hills which rise out of the sea around Phi Phi. We talked about our dogs, Harry and Sally. Troy had always loved dogs and he really missed them while we were away. Whenever Troy was out, Harry would keep guard in the bedroom at our place, looking through the curtains onto the street.

On the way back to our room, we asked directions to Tonsai at the front desk.

Little did we know that at that moment, over 1000 kilometres away, two giant geological plates which usually moved only a few inches a year had just collided, smashing a thousand-kilometre-long rift into the floor of the Indian Ocean and causing a massive earthquake.

It was 9 am when we set out for the forty-five minute walk. The track led from the back of the resort, where many of the locals who worked in the hotel had their homes. They lived simply, and many of them waved to us as we wound our way through the increasingly unkempt grass and onto a jungle path.

Thankfully we were both wearing runners, as finding the right track was not as easy as we had thought and it was quite rough and steep. As we started the climb up the mountain, Troy told me to go in front so he could catch me if I slipped backwards. Even though we were both fit, it was hard work in the morning sun, and the humid air made conditions oppressive. Troy was in training but he still struggled. I needed to rest every now and then.

The Thai jungle was quiet, and we could hear nothing but the sounds of our own feet tramping dead leaves on the path. We had no idea of the magnitude of the disaster unfolding throughout Asia. The displacement caused by the earthquake had raised the sea level by several metres, causing a ripple of waves to spread outwards across the Indian Ocean. Thirty minutes after the quake, the first of these waves – by now twenty metres high – had smashed into Sumatra, surging over 800 metres inland and killing close to 200,000 people in fifteen minutes.

Going down the hill was a lot easier than the trip up, and we emerged from the jungle and stepped onto the rocks of Tonsai Bay at exactly 10 am, covered in sweat. Just twenty kilometres offshore the tsunami front had already been building up force for over an hour. What should have taken us forty-five minutes to walk had ended up being more like sixty, and I often wonder what would have happened if we'd had a local guide with us. Would we have arrived earlier and been up at the Viewpoint by now?

The track from the jungle emerged onto the bay inlet about 400 metres from the main beach of Phi Phi, with our destination of the Viewpoint a further hundred metres behind the beach. The scene before us was magnificent – you could not imagine a more beautiful place. The southern part of Phi Phi Don Island is basically two mountains joined by a narrow neck of land, creating two bays and a giant beach that stretches around the island. Bungalows, shops and cafes sat under palm trees along the edge of the beach, while the larger hotels and street markets were packed in a little village behind it. There are no roads and very few tuktuks on the island, and tens of thousands flock there every year to lap up the simple life. It really is paradise.

We had visited the village two days before by longtail boat and the beach had been packed. Now, because it was Boxing Day, the beach was not as crowded as it had been earlier that week, but things were still busy. All along the edge of the beach Thai fishermen were mending their nets and women were tending to their young children.

Troy held my hand and helped me over the rocks leading to the beach as we wove in and out of the Thai fishing huts. I can remember Troy looking at the huts made out of lashed bamboo and commenting on how happy everyone looked. As soon as the Thai people saw Troy their faces lit up. Troy's smile was contagious, and when he flashed his big grin at them they laughed, pointing at his red hair, or maybe it was his height, or just his nature they responded to. Despite being shy back home, Troy loved talking to people in Thailand.

Troy helped me down onto the sand and we walked along the beach. Tourists played in the water, fishermen hauled nets onto their boats, and the longboat taxis which ferried people between islands queued up in rows waiting for tourists to jump on board.

At this stage, the tsunami was already at the mouth of the bay behind us, but even though it was so close, we still could not see it. While it was on the ocean, the tsunami was a huge body of water rather than a wave, but the power behind it would be unleashed when it hit land or shallow water. Behind it, hundreds of thousands of people were already fighting for their lives on the shores of Indonesia and Malaysia. I still find it hard to accept how one minute things can be perfect and then the next, in a matter of seconds, they can turn to disaster. How could no one know the wave was coming? A simple warning would have cleared the beach in minutes.

We walked holding hands and everything seemed peaceful and calm. Then I noticed that the water's edge had begun to retreat quickly back into the bay. Other witnesses said later that the water went so far back they could see fish flapping on the sand, but all I saw was the water being sucked out to sea and suddenly recoiling as it hit the tsunami front.

People always want to know what was it like just before the tsunami hit, but it is almost impossible to describe. A tsunami doesn't just 'hit' you, it kind of sneaks up and then totally obliterates you. It's almost like there is no beginning. Some of the footage I have seen on the internet is misleading, because no camera is capable of capturing the total power of a tsunami. It's like nothing else, like no other experience.

Contrary to what many people believe, a tsunami does not hit like a massive surf wave in one strike. It builds momentum and floods up onto the beach, more like a river which has burst its banks than an actual wave. Unlike a river, however, a tsunami has the force of the whole ocean behind it, so when it starts to 'flood', it does so with tremendous power and it doesn't stop.

At first we were more shocked than scared – it was like when a big wave hits at the beach and everyone scuttles away with their towels and belongings to stop from getting wet. But as the water continued to flow, Troy and I looked at each other a little uncertainly and began to run up the beach.

Running across the sand, I began to sense how serious this was going to be. Further around the beach, where the tide had first hit, I could see canoes moving really quickly on top of the water as though they were powered by outboards. It was then I realised that they were well and truly up where the beach used to be and that they were heading straight for the main block of hotels. Just seconds ago there had been people lazing on the beach – now about five metres of water was carrying everything in its path.

I looked across at Troy who had seen the same thing. But before we could acknowledge what was happening, we heard the noise. The quiet peaceful scene of minutes ago was suddenly immersed in what sounded like a distant jet plane approaching. And seconds behind the noise came the first main body of water. The only way I can describe it is like a huge black wall of water and debris rising out of the sea, growing bigger and bigger. There was nothing normal about the colour or the contents of this wave. Troy looked at me and grabbed my hand, hauling me up the beach towards one of the bungalows on stilts. I think we were hoping we could climb up onto their balcony and let the water pass beneath.

Everything happened so fast, it is hard to recall. There was no time to panic, we just acted. We clambered up on the bungalow's balcony as high as we could and, for a brief moment, looked out to face the massive wall of black water about to engulf us.

Time froze. How could this be happening? We were on our honeymoon. Two minutes ago we were walking peacefully along the beach with the world at our feet, and now we were about to be swept away.

Sometimes, life comes down to a matter of seconds. I held Troy's hand as tightly as I could. Troy was a strong athlete and I trusted in him physically and even then, in high danger, I felt Troy was strong enough to help us both. I knew my best bet was to hold onto him. Seconds before the full force hit, I felt Troy's arms around me, almost as though he were trying to lift me above the approaching water. That's when I lost it and started to scream, 'Oh, my God, this is not going to stop!'

As the water hit, Troy made one last effort to lift me above the wave. But the water crashed onto us, smashing the hut in front of the bungalow to pieces, sending it careering straight into my face. For a moment, I could still feel Troy's hands pushing me upward and then, with a cyclone-like force, I was ripped away from his grasp and tumbled into a sea of debris and water.

Being in the wave itself was like being sucked down a giant plughole, twisted and turned, battered by debris which was caught up in the wave; I had no idea where I was going. The force of the wave was so strong, I couldn't even think of fighting against it, so I just let go. As I did so a thought came into my head: 'I can't believe I'm going to die on my honeymoon.' In my mind I saw a picture of Troy's face and I wondered what he was going to do without me. I kept reaching out for him but instead I just felt more water. At this stage I had been underwater for about a minute, and then suddenly the water calmed and I thought to myself, 'Okay, I can get my head above it now.' But then the real wave hit. The first had only been the beginning – the second was three times stronger and carried with it all the debris from the village.

Suddenly I was propelled forward into total darkness. I was metres under the water and I could feel objects cutting into me, gashing against my flesh, ripping at random into my legs and arms. I tried to raise my arms to protect my face, but the force was so great I couldn't even do that. Eventually I had no choice but go with it, fighting was useless. I thought one last time of Troy, and with my lungs bursting, I fell into unconsciousness.

I don't know how long I was underwater, but it was long enough for me to travel about 600 metres in the wave. Being underwater for several minutes was bad enough, but being under water which has been pushed by a magnitude 9.0 earthquake, with the contents of an entire village being pummelled around you – I still don't understand how I survived. My head was not above the wave at any stage; I was under metres of water the whole time.

I'm not quite sure how I regained consciousness. But when I did, I was overcome with calmness. I could feel twisted metal and wood around me everywhere, and somehow I knew I had to get air. To my surprise, my feet made contact with something solid and I was able to stand. A few seconds longer and I think I would have passed out again. There was a balcony above me, and with the last of my strength, I looked up and started to climb, using the debris to gain footings. As I raised my head above the level of the balcony I saw two people and screamed for help, but they just looked at me and shook their heads. Then, from nowhere, a hand reached down into the water and pulled me upward into the air and onto the balcony of a hotel. I coughed and spewed water, and for the first time in minutes my lungs were again filled with air.

The first words I uttered were, 'Is Troy okay?'

It was 10:45 am.

Chapter 2

26 DECEMBER 2004:
The Aftermath

The hand that reached down into the wreckage belonged to a British tourist. He took one look at me, and I could see by his expression that I was not in a good way. My head was throbbing in pain and my eye was so swollen I could cup it in my hand. I lay on the balcony in a pool of blood, which I soon realised was my own. Tentatively I felt behind my knee which was extremely painful, but instead of skin I felt only flesh. I looked at my hand covered in blood and then at the rest of my body which was a mess of gaping cuts.

From the balcony I had my first brief glimpse of the devastation below. At this stage, I was still unsure exactly what had happened. To one side of us the water was peaceful but it was obvious how forceful it had been – whole palm trees had been uprooted, bungalows floated at irregular angles in the water and the air was filled with the sounds of screaming people.

Once I got my bearings, I realised I was quite high above the ground and the water of the tsunami was settling below. I had washed up about 600 metres from the beach and had come to rest on a pile of rubble which had built up around one of the few hotels still standing. The hotel was at the foot of the mountain which led to the lookout, and later I wondered if this was another factor which may have saved my life. Because the debris of the wave had nowhere else to go when it hit the mountain, it began to pile up and divert the flow of water over the narrow strip of land that linked the two sides of the island and out into the opposite bay. For the shopkeepers and small business owners, however, this was a disaster. When the wave hit, the entire contents of their shops, and in many cases the shops themselves, were washed across the island and out into the bay.

My daze was broken by the urgency of the Englishman's voice.

'There's another wave coming,' he yelled. 'Run to the Viewpoint while you can.' He ran off down the stairs and started to make his way to the steps which led to the lookout.

As it turned out, there was no third wave, but people were so panicked that anyone who could walk was rushing to higher ground. The Viewpoint was the highest point on the island and it seemed the only safe place to be. Luckily for those of us stranded in this hotel, the water around the back had subsided and I managed to drag myself down the stairs and over to the path. I looked frantically for Troy, half expecting his face to bob up at any moment. Dragging my bad leg behind me, I began to stumble towards the steps to the lookout.

For the next hour, it was literally every man for himself. People pushed past others in a desperate bid to get to higher ground or find lost loved ones. I was no different, and had my leg been okay

I would have done anything to find Troy. As it was, I was moving so slowly that I was blocking the narrow path. I don't blame them, but people literally pushed me over in their haste. Having never experienced a tsunami before, no one knew what to expect, and anyone who could move wasn't hanging around to find out.

Behind me, I could still hear the desperate screams of people searching for loved ones, but by now a strange calm had overcome the island. The water was still, slowly subsiding back into the ocean. For a brief moment I looked back and all I could see were the rooftops of buildings which had managed to stay standing. The rest was water.

The concrete steps up to the lookout are about a kilometre long, and under normal circumstances it might be a thirty-minute walk. Surrounded by jungle on either side, the steps are very steep but wide enough for two people to walk side by side. I had been on the steps almost an hour and had only managed to go about twenty metres. Around me, people of all nations rushed upward, some carrying babies in their arms, others screaming the names of family and friends. Below, the village on Tonsai Bay had been overcome by a weird calm. The floodwaters were slowly subsiding, but literally everything in their path was gone, just wiped away. Where once there had been huts, buildings and people, there was now only sand, dotted with pools of water and giant piles of debris.

By late morning, I was exhausted and losing blood. No one stopped to help me, and once I knew I was out of reach of the water, I could only think of one thing: Troy.

Desperate, I lay on the side of the steps yelling his name, pleading with people to stop and help me look for him. I kept telling myself that if I had survived, surely Troy had as well. Like me, he would be making his way up to the top of the Viewpoint.

By now my right eye was completely swollen shut and I could only see out of the left. I must have looked a total wreck, covered in blood and screaming Troy's name. It felt like an eternity before anyone stopped, but eventually a British dive instructor who had not been on the beach when the wave hit came over and offered me water. I was so thirsty I gulped down what he offered.

I was about to get up and move on when he said, 'You can't go on. You really need a doctor. I'll go and get someone.'

'No,' I screamed. 'I have to find my husband.'

'Look, you're in a really bad way. You need help.'

Suddenly I vomited on myself, and I think it was a mixture of the salt water I had swallowed and the fear I felt. The thought that I might be dying crept into my head.

I was dazed and not thinking straight when a slightly built Thai man walked up to us, spoke for a moment to the dive instructor and then leant down and lifted me onto his shoulder. It turned out he was a doctor and was taking people to his house. My head was spinning, like one of those movies where the person is on drugs. I couldn't focus on anything and the pain in my body was the only thing stopping me from blacking out. I didn't want to go anywhere, but I had no strength to fight. The Thai doctor and the British dive instructor carried me for about ten minutes, away from the Viewpoint track. The British man kept saying, 'You're going to be okay, just hold on.' I couldn't work out why he would say that. Of course I was going to be okay. It was Troy I was worried about.

After about ten minutes we reached the doctor's house and they took me around the back of the house and laid me down on the balcony. His wife and three daughters were there but otherwise the house was empty. The Thai doctor then came out and offered me two tablets. I didn't know what they were and didn't want to take them, but he assured me they would stop the pain.

It was then I started to freak. This didn't feel right. Where were all the other injured people? Why had he bought me here? It seemed strange to be at his house on my own since I had been surrounded by people just minutes ago. The doctor came in and started to take my clothes off. He started with my shoes, left my shorts on and then peeled off my top. The pain was unbearable. The debris in the wave had cut into my skin and pushed my shirt deep into the wounds, so peeling it off meant each of the wounds was reopened.

Every fear I had ever had was there at that moment. I was in massive pain, I could not find my husband, I was half naked, disorientated and alone with a stranger who was administering medical treatment to me.

In hindsight, that man probably saved my life. Many people died from infection after the wave, and had he not treated the wounds he could see, I might have joined them.

I lay recovering on a mattress on the Thai man's balcony for at least two hours. During that time he brought in others and treated them too, and I began to hear snippets of what had happened that day, listening to people telling their stories. But even at this stage it was unclear how much damage the wave had caused and what enormous loss of life there had been.

By now it was mid afternoon, and what was clear was that all those who had survived had walked up to the Viewpoint. So with renewed strength, I decided to get up and make my way there as best I could to find my husband.

When the dive instructor returned, I said to him, 'I have to go now. I have to find Troy.' He must have been able to tell from my voice that I was serious so he didn't argue but helped me stand up.

As we walked past the Thai doctor, he asked, 'Where are you going? You need to stay and rest.'

'I have to find my husband,' I said.

'But your face, it is bad, you must stay here.'

I looked straight at the British dive instructor. 'You have to take me back to where the others are.' It was not a plea but a command. The Thai doctor tried to talk me out of it, but I was going, no matter what. I didn't even stop to put my shoes on. Dragging my bad leg behind me, I began to stumble back to the track up to the Viewpoint.

In the end no one tried to stop me. By now even more people had been brought in to see the Thai doctor, and they were just too busy.

For a while my leg was fine, but the further I walked the more pain I felt. While the doctor had managed to cover the major cuts on my arms and body, he had missed the biggest one at the back of my knee.

The British man took me to the track where he had met up with some other English guys. I sat with them for about an hour, asking people as they passed if they had seen Troy.

After a while I asked one of the Englishmen if he would go up to the Viewpoint for me and look for Troy. I gave him a sign which I made with a bit of cardboard and a texta someone had. I wrote:

Troy Broadbridge 24
Westerner red hair
Looking for Trisha

When the Englishman returned forty minutes later with no news of Troy, I thanked him and started up the track on my own. For the next hour, I managed to half crawl, half walk up the stairs, driven only by the thought that Troy would be up there to meet me. I was barefoot and bleeding, but nothing was going to stop me.

It had been over four hours since the wave had hit, and all along the path people had made makeshift camps, waiting for relatives and friends to walk past them. Taking one small step at a time and then dragging my bad leg behind me, I kept calling out Troy's name, but my voice was lost in the chaos. The wound behind my leg was deep, and although I couldn't see my face one whole side felt like it had been smashed with a baseball bat. My insides hurt, and even in all that chaos I wondered if I could still have children. To keep me going, I tried diverting my mind from the pain, but the thoughts that surfaced were equally as challenging.

I reached the top of the mountain around 4 pm. I was totally exhausted and unable to go any further. By now the lookout was packed with people, many of them injured, and filled with the sounds of raw emotion. Hundreds more were crammed all the way down the track, trying to get to higher ground in the fear that another wave would strike.

I heard a voice behind me asking if I was okay. 'You need to take water, here, drink this.' The voice belonged to a Canadian woman, who along with her family had walked to the Viewpoint from the other side of the island.

The Canadian family tried to make me comfortable where I was lying as I told them my story and gave them a description of Troy. I was still in shock and delirious. Although I had stopped bleeding, my cuts were agonising and I couldn't see from one eye. But even more painful were the screams of people as they found out news about their loved ones. Sometimes the yells were of joy and other times you could tell the news was bad.

Around me where I lay, about a hundred people were huddled in little groups. Despite the care and concern shown by the Canadian family, I felt so alone. I was surrounded by people, but none of them was Troy.

At one stage I heard the screams of a woman as she was reunited with her husband. I just lay there and watched as she held onto him like she was never going to let go. I hated myself for the emotions that rose in me. But I kept thinking, why them? Why not me? There were moments of terror when I thought that perhaps Troy hadn't made it, and then there were moments of peace, when I focused on how it would be when we were reunited. I would hold him so tightly and kiss him, and I would never let him go again.

Chapter 3

27 DECEMBER 2004: *Leaving Phi Phi*

At first light, a western volunteer came up and said that injured people should be taken to the bottom of the Viewpoint from where they were being evacuated by helicopter to Krabi on the mainland. The evacuation had begun the night before but they'd had to cease when it became dark. After a short consultation with the Canadian family, we decided that since Troy hadn't made it up to the Viewpoint, he was most likely down the mountain waiting to be evacuated. So with the help of the Canadians I began the long descent.

The trip down was painful, but I was driven by the thought that Troy might be at the evacuation point. All the way down the mountain, my eyes were darting to everyone. I had to find Troy. Even though I knew he would never leave Phi Phi Island without me, I still kept my focus on finding him to avoid having to think about the alternative. 'Do you think Troy is down here?' I kept asking. The Canadians were non-committal, and I think their main motive was to get me to safety, but as soon as we reached the bottom I insisted on going over to the ferry wharf to see if we could spot Troy. There was a huge queue of people who didn't need medical evacuation waiting to go back to the mainland. But once again I was disappointed; there was no sign of my husband at all.

As they carried me across to where the choppers were leaving from, I caught a glimpse of what used to be Tonsai Bay. Virtually everything was gone. The water had subsided but in its place where once there had been a village there were now random piles of rubble. Although it had been less than twenty-four hours, the stench of dead bodies was already strong in the air.

The military-style makeshift hospital consisted of a line of mattresses laid side by side on the ground. The volunteers tried to make me lie down but my leg was too painful so I half-sat on the mattress while the Canadians gave me fresh water and a little food.

Not far away, helicopters were landing and taking people away. I soon realised I was in line to be taken away too. I started to panic, screaming that I did not want to go on the helicopter, but the noise from the helicopter engines was deafening and no one could hear. On the mattress across from me, an old lady was lying very still while her daughter held her hand. She had a mask over her face. As the helicopter noise receded, I began to hear what the daughter was saying. Even though she was speaking in Thai, I could feel the emotion.

The helicopter flights came back every ten or so minutes, and every time a helicopter arrived the down draft of the blades caused the sand to fly up and blow into our exposed wounds. Just about everyone there had cuts similar to mine. I can't begin to describe what it was like to see those wounds fill with sand knowing that at some stage it would all have to be washed out.

While I waited, a tent-like cover was placed over me – a sheet draped over two poles. Several aid workers had arrived that morning and one was trying to assist me, but as soon as the helicopter took off, the makeshift leg cover blew away and once again my face and wounds were filled with sand. The pole landed on my foot. I screamed in pain but no one could hear me. I tried to reach down to pull it off but I could not move my body. When a nurse finally came and unwrapped the two worst wounds which had been covered by the Canadians, I was shocked to see how bad they were. Even though they had been bound, the cuts in my arm had gone right through to the bone.

I realised I had to leave Phi Phi Island to get proper medical attention. A volunteer told me that a man of Troy's description had left the island the night before, so that made leaving a little easier, even though I still felt he would not have left without me. The Canadians seemed relieved to know I was going to get help and they promised they would continue to look for Troy.

It was only about 9 am when I boarded a chopper to the Thai mainland. The helicopter evacuation was like a scene out of a Vietnam movie. As I was being loaded on, other westerners were being physically pushed off as they tried to get on board. Most of the people with me were Thais. I really felt for them, they were leaving everything behind. It wasn't just that they had lost family and friends – many of them had lost everything. All they had in the world was the clothes they wore on that chopper.

As we took off, I could not look down. I was trying to hold on but there were no handles. I was petrified that the door was going to fly open and we would all be sucked out. I put my head behind the back of a Thai man who was sitting next to me and tried to close my eyes but I couldn't. The trip was only fifteen minutes, but a lady lying on the floor next to us died during the flight. I don't know how I knew she was dead, but I knew.

For the whole flight, I kept thinking about my reunion with Troy and how we would share stories of what had happened to us overnight. I dreamt of holding him and kissing him. I would tell him I wanted to start our family now.

When the helicopter landed in Krabi, I was put on a stretcher and carried across to a Thai ambulance, which was more like an old ute than a medical emergency vehicle. With sirens wailing, the ambulance took off, leaving me reeling in pain with each bump. Except for a Thai doctor, I was alone in the ambulance, and I kept asking the man, 'Where are we going? Where are we going?' All he kept saying was one word, over and over: 'Hospital, hospital, hospital.'

When we reached the Krabi hospital, I was taken out of the ambulance onto a waiting wheelchair. News of the tsunami had hit the mainland by now and crowds had gathered outside the hospital, waiting for relatives and friends, or maybe just out of curiosity. Having been surrounded by injured people for the last twenty-four hours I was used to the sight, but as we got out of the ambulance, the crowd let out an 'Ooohh' and almost took a step backwards. I must have looked awful.

I waited outside the hospital on my own for forty-five minutes. None of the nurses spoke English and they kept trying to give me injections that I refused. I was alone and had no idea what was going on, and I was terrified of accepting any needles that I hadn't seen come out of a sterile package. There were others waiting to go in, and the crowds had gathered around us, watching as we were lined up to go into the hospital. A doctor came up and placed a wrist band on me with an outline picture of a human body on it. Next he drew small lines on the picture to represent the cuts I had which needed stitching.

At about 10 am a volunteer came and wheeled me into the hospital, down a long corridor with people sitting against the walls waiting to be treated. The place was packed and full of screaming people, like the casualty ward in one of those war movies. As we passed each room, I looked in to see if Troy was there.

At the end of the corridor we entered a huge room filled with people lying on small mats. On the far side there were offices and phones. The volunteer took me out of the wheelchair and placed me in a plastic chair, telling me she would be back soon. I looked around at the carnage. People were wailing in pain and others were lying stunned while volunteers did their best to change bandages and patch people up.

Across the other end of the building behind a glass office wall sat a tall man with red hair. 'Troy! Troy!' I yelled. But he was too far away to hear. 'Troy!' I yelled in a weak voice. I was desperate to get to him, but there was no way to cross the room. I convinced myself it was Troy, but when he finally turned around it was not Troy at all. Yet my hopes were lifted and I felt sure I would find him soon.

Volunteers were walking around with signs on them indicating the languages they spoke. I had about six of them out looking for

Troy. An English woman named Judy came up to me and asked if she could help. I told her my story, and as I did, she started to cry. From that moment Judy became my main source of emotional and practical support, and she looked after me and helped me enormously.

Judy helped me get across to the phones, where I waited for about ten minutes before it was my turn. Up until now it had not even occurred to me what my and Troy's parents were going through. It was about 11 am in Krabi, which made it about 3 pm back in Melbourne.

I rang home and Mum told me they had not heard from Troy. At the time I had no idea how much they knew in Melbourne about the scale of the tsunami disaster and how much pressure they had been under, waiting for news. But I was not interested in talking about myself at that stage, my mind was totally focused on finding Troy. Because I was only able to speak on the phone for a short period of time, Judy gave Mum her mobile number and Mum rang Judy straight back to hear what had happened to me and how bad my injuries were.

Kaye's story

We were out at Southbank the day that news of the tsunami hit Melbourne. My other daughter Tracey rang us as soon as she heard.

'Mum, have you heard the news? There's been a giant tsunami over in Thailand where Trisha and Troy are.'

At first I kept telling myself to try and be calm, but as we were driving home a news flash came over the radio, saying that over 300 people had been killed on Phi Phi Island and the death toll was expected to rise into the thousands.

Tom was stunned. He started shaking and had to pull over to the side of the road. I have never felt so powerless. Suddenly after a day of fun at the casino and a lovely lunch, there we were sitting in our car on the side of the road, hearing the news that our daughter and son-in-law may well have been washed away in a killer wave on their honeymoon.

When we regained composure we rushed home to get hold of Trisha's travel plans to see if she was actually on Phi Phi when the wave hit and to find a number to contact her.

The next four hours were hell. We tried and tried to ring the hotel where Trisha and Troy were staying, but on the few occasions we managed to get through, it was so difficult to speak to the Thai desk clerk that we couldn't get a clear picture of where Trisha and Troy were. All we knew was that they were not in their room, but they were on the island.

It occurred to me that perhaps Troy may have tried to call the Broadbridges so I put through a call to Wayne and Pam. Pam is one of the most positive people I have ever met, and despite not having heard from Troy, she was still full of hope. 'It'll be okay,' she kept saying.

When I hung up the phone from the Broadbridges I slumped down into a chair and started my phone-side vigil, waiting for the call that I thought would never come. In times like this the hardest part is not the situation itself but the not knowing. You don't know what emotion is right, so instead you just feel them all. Even more challenging was the fact that the phone never stopped ringing, and it seemed every minute someone was knocking at the door to find out what was going on.

By now the news had spread and Trisha's brothers Tim and Trent and her sister Tracey had arrived at home to begin the horrible waiting game.

We sat glued to the news, watching the footage as the tsunami began to get more and more exposure. The first pictures we saw were from a resort in Thailand where the water literally flooded up out of the sea and filled the first floor of a hotel. I think anyone who saw that original footage will understand what I mean when I say it was like watching a movie rather than real life.

As news started to filter through, we discovered there was a hotline to ring for relatives of people travelling over in Asia. My son Tim was the first to get on the phone. We expected the message would simply say that it was too early for details and names to be made available and that we should ring back later. Instead the hotline contained the worst news imaginable. Rather than reassuring words and glossing over the seriousness of the situation, the embassy advised that the situation in Asia was highly critical and if we had not heard anything by now, we should 'prepare for the worst'.

I am not an optimistic person at the best of times, but when I heard that news I felt in my heart of hearts that we had lost Troy and Trisha. It had now been over twenty-four hours since the wave had hit and we had heard nothing.

I was exhausted when the phone rang for about the tenth

time that day, and I was expecting to hear the voice of another friend or relative checking up on the situation. I picked up the phone and before I heard anything, my heart jumped at the slight delay you get sometimes when a call is international.

The next words I heard were the most bittersweet to ever reach my ears.

'Mum, it's me, Trisha. Has Troy contacted you yet?'

There was no easy way to answer that question. One part of me was trying to hide my elation, and the other was working up the courage to deliver the news which I knew would devastate my daughter.

'No sweetheart, no one has heard anything yet.'

I was bursting to ask her how she was, but it seemed at the time that was not important. By now everyone in the house was silent and listening in to my conversation and as soon as Dad heard the words 'Trisha', he started running around the house yelling, 'She's okay. Trisha's alive! She's okay.'

There was silence on the phone for a minute and then, as only Trisha can, she started giving orders. 'Mum, you have to come over right now and help me look for Troy.' She gave me the details of where she was, and before I knew it I was checking the airlines to book a ticket over to Thailand.

But before I did that I had one phone call to make. It was to the Broadbridges. I have no idea how they managed to keep their strength after hearing the news that Trisha was okay but Troy had not yet been found. Before the phone call we had almost given up hope, and had even talked about burying Trisha and Troy together in Adelaide so they could be with each other.

I will never forget how strong and positive Pam and Wayne were when I told them the news. They are incredible people.

The news that Troy had not contacted home hit me hard. It had now been thirty-six hours since the wave hit and with every passing hour it became less and less likely Troy would be found.

Judy went to look again around the hospital for him and found out there was a shuttle bus to the Maritime Hotel where most of the westerners were being taken. That afternoon I was transferred by bus to the hotel and Judy came with me. I was told a representative from the Australian Embassy would be there to meet me.

The Maritime Hotel was much calmer than the hospital. The function room was filled with westerners from all over the world trying to get home. Judy helped me walk in and placed me on a seat next to a British couple. In the next chair was a New Zealand man who offered me the money to fly home if I needed it. Perhaps most incredibly, later that day I met a young girl who lived three doors down from my parents in Melbourne. Judy stayed with me for about an hour and helped me fill out a set of forms which had been issued by the Thai police.

Within a couple of hours Judy had received a message back from Mum to say that she could not come out to meet me straightaway because she needed to get a passport – she had never been overseas before – so my sister Tracey would be coming instead.

Judy said she would pick Tracey up at the airport and bring her to meet me in the morning. Judy's partner spent some time looking for Troy at the ferry, and also helped by bringing me clean clothes.

While I settled in to wait for Tracey in the foyer of the Maritime Hotel, I met a young boy and his father who were on the chairs next to me. The father looked in total shock and could not speak.

The little boy came over and sat next to me.

'Are you okay?' I asked.

He said, 'Yes, but my mum died in the wave.'

He was about seven years old and spoke with an English accent.

'We were on the beach, and when the water came, my dad pushed me up a palm tree and told me to climb. I was looking down and I saw the water push Mum into the tree.'

The boy's father lifted his head from between his hands and his dark eyes stared at his son. At that moment his phone rang. The little boy reached over and took it from his dad's lap. His dad was just shaking and could not do a thing.

I have often thought of that little boy since. Looking at the dad, you could see the absolute pain he felt at losing his wife. And yet the son was behaving on the surface is if nothing had happened. It seems to be something kids can do. For the first time in two days, I found myself thinking about someone other than Troy.

At about six o'clock that evening, a bus arrived to take people who wanted to go to the airport where there were free flights to Bangkok. From where I was sitting I could see everyone scrambling to try and get on, like frantic school kids pushing onto a school bus. That night, many buses came to take people away, while those of us who were waiting for others had to stay.

At about 9 pm I realised everyone I had met that day had gone. I felt very alone. It was the second night since the tsunami and I had been sure this was the day I would find Troy. As the night dragged on, I started thinking that perhaps he was in a coma somewhere, still alive but unable to communicate. I could not bring myself to believe that he was dead.

That night I was overwhelmed by feelings of massive guilt. I felt I should have stayed on Phi Phi Island to look for Troy. I became convinced that everyone back home would hate me. To this day I can't reconcile leaving Troy behind. Before I knew it, my mind started playing a loop of thoughts. 'How could this possibly happen to us? How could it happen now, when things were going so well? Why were we on the beach? What if I hadn't walked so slowly? What if we had lost our way or turned back? Why had the wave taken me and Troy so far apart? Was he lying somewhere unconscious? Was he thinking of me, desperate to contact me? Was he in pain? Was he still alive?'

For twenty-four hours the questions did not stop, they bounced around in my head relentlessly. It was the onset of an emotional state of guilt and self-blame which would not leave me for months.

In the function room a television tuned to CNN was playing footage of the tsunami and the devastation around the world. I could hardly watch it – I could not handle hearing how bad things were – but I glanced at the screen whenever I heard familiar landmarks being mentioned. I caught the words Phi Phi Island and looked up in the hope I might see Troy. Instead there was footage of a girl being loaded onto a helicopter. She looked so afraid, but before I could even begin to feel sorry for her, I realised the girl on the television was me. I was being helped into the helicopter by the Canadian man.

I hadn't seen myself in a mirror at all, and now I had to see what I looked like. It took me ten minutes to hobble to the bathroom, and it was a stranger's face that looked back at me. One eye was completely swollen, and because I hadn't slept, my 'good' eye was totally bloodshot. I had dirt all over me and sand and twigs stuck in my hair. I wondered if I would ever look like me again.

It was as if, even now, the story of what had happened was out of my control. I couldn't recognise myself in the mirror, and I couldn't recognise myself as someone who had survived a tsunami. What the wave had taken from my identity in a physical sense was much easier to deal with than what it had taken from my identity in a emotional way.

I hobbled back to the function room and started rocking in my chair, distressed and crying. All I could think of was getting hold of a phone, to hear a familiar voice again. I made my way slowly over to the information desk where a man named Stuart asked if he could help me.

'Can I please borrow your phone?' I asked, 'I have to call home.'

Seeing my distress, Stuart lent me his mobile phone without hesitation. First I tried Mum, but I couldn't get through, so I texted her instead. I tried a few other numbers I knew off by heart, hoping to get through to someone, but no one was answering.

The next thing I knew a text message had popped up on Stuart's phone from Mum: 'Tracey on her way over.'

I texted back the following message: 'I am so scared and alone. Everyone has gone, please help.'

Stuart told me I could hang onto his phone for a while in case someone texted me back.

A lady gave me a valium and helped me lie down, as I could not lie on the floor without assistance due to my injuries. By now I was bursting to hear from one of Troy's friends. I was sick with the thought that they may blame me for what had happened. I texted Daniel Bell, one of Troy's best friends. Troy and Belly played together at Melbourne and had become really close when Belly took the locker next to Troy's. I had no idea what I was going to say to him. I felt responsible, and I knew how much Belly loved Troy. My message said: 'I'm so sorry, I promise I will keep looking for Troy and I won't come home without him.'

Belly's text back said: 'It's okay. We'll find him, and I am so glad to hear you are okay.'

To see those words from Belly meant a huge amount to me. To know that one of Troy's closest friends was glad I was alive when I felt swamped with guilt helped me feel that maybe people back home wouldn't blame me for leaving Phi Phi without Troy.

During the evening several people sent me text messages, telling me things would be okay and that everyone back home was hoping and praying we would find Troy. But even so, that night was full of pain. I could hardly breathe. Every hour or so, faxes would come through from the hospital with lists of patients who had been admitted, and the staff would pin them to a large board at the end of the foyer. I couldn't stop reading them, over and over again, in case I had missed a message from Troy. But each time there was nothing.

The enormity of what had happened was starting to sink in. I stayed awake most of the night, watching as new people came into the hotel, hoping Troy would be one of them. Now even my good eye was swollen and sore from crying and I could hardly stop shaking. I looked blankly at people as they entered, willing their hair to change colour or for them to be taller, trying to turn them into Troy.

Chapter 4

28 DECEMBER 2004:
The Maritime Hotel

In the morning I was woken from a very light sleep by Stuart. People had been leaving messages on his phone for me all night.

The most urgent was from Jim Stynes. He had managed to speak to Terri Bracks, the wife of Victorian premier Steve Bracks, and Mum's passport was being fast-tracked so she would be on the way over soon after Tracey.

I had known Jim for over nine years through the Reach Foundation which Jim had co-founded to inspire, support and motivate young people. Jim had also played football for Melbourne and was still involved with the club. Troy and I had become close friends with Jim and his wife, Sam, and their daughter Matisse was a flower girl at our wedding.

I used Stuart's phone to return Jim's call, and amazingly, I got through straight away. I briefly told him what had happened. He asked me about my injuries and I told him I thought my face was scarred for life. Jim was very calm, as he tends to be in a crisis, and he told me that Reach would send Emeli over to help me. Emeli and I had worked together at Reach for years. She had been a bridesmaid at my wedding and was one of my closest friends. Jim also told me he had spoken to Troy's parents and that there were people out everywhere looking for Troy. I told Jim that my sister Tracey was already on the way over. The whole conversation didn't feel real. I was still in shock, I think, and my speech was confused. Nothing that I could say could explain what was happening and I felt frustrated that I couldn't get across the full picture.

When Jim hung up I was totally worn out and devoid of emotion. It was as if I had shut down, emotionally and mentally.

I noticed in a corner of the function room people were using a computer. I managed to hobble over there and saw they were online. I waited until the computer was free and sat down in the hope that perhaps Troy had somehow sent me an email.

I opened Hotmail and typed in my password. First I checked our joint email but there was nothing from Troy. There was a message from our friend Paige Davies: 'The wedding was amazing, thank you so much for inviting me. I have made a disk of all the photos and sent it off to you.' I sat for ages just staring at the screen, wondering what to write back. That email seemed to be from another life. I thought of sending a group email, but I had absolutely no idea what to say. In the end I did nothing.

Next I tried my uni address, but again there was nothing. In one last hope, I tried Troy's own address, but it too was empty.

After this I rang Emeli on Stuart's phone. I wondered if I should warn her about the extent of my injuries, and to let her know that it was okay for her to come. I kept wondering if I was overdramatising this whole thing. Suddenly three people were coming from overseas to help: Tracey, Mum, and now Emeli too. Dad won't fly, and Mum had never even been overseas before. But she was determined not to stay behind. I still could not grasp how bad things were, and I thought that Troy would find it funny when he found me because I had created such a commotion.

I ended up using all the credit on Stuart's phone. If I'd had any money I would have given it to him, but under the circumstances he really didn't care. People were very kind to me.

At about 9 am the trauma nurses came in to assess people. They saw the back of my leg and noticed it was infected. I had gone for two days without a bandage, and although some of my other wounds had been covered, many were open and weeping, and I had not yet had a full wash. The cuts on my arms were full of pus, but the back of my leg was even worse. I couldn't see it but I could feel how open and pussy it was, and it had even started to smell. The nurses wanted me to go back to hospital but I kept telling them that Tracey was coming soon so I couldn't go yet.

I was glad Tracey was the one arriving first. There is something very special in the bond between sisters. We are both strong women, but we can do or say anything to each other, because at the end of the day she will always be my sister and I love her. Even though we find it difficult at times to show each other how much we care, we would each be the first to stick up for the other in times of trouble.

The Thai nurses were almost at the point of holding me down to stick a tetanus needle into me, but I was fighting back. Had it gone on much longer someone would have gotten hurt, and it would not have been me. I know they were only trying to do their job, but Troy and I had had all our injections before we left Australia, and I still did not want to take the risk of being injected with a less than sterile needle.

Despite my protests and the commotion around me, when Tracey came into the room with Judy, she walked straight past. She did not even recognise me.

'Tracey!' I called out. She turned and looked at me, and the expression on her face said it all. There could be no happiness in these reunions. I knew Tracey was glad I was alive, but she was shocked at the extent of my injuries. And I felt wiped of all emotion. The last thing on my mind was feeling happy to see her. All I wanted was to find Troy.

Tracey's story

I knew I was in a no-win situation with Trisha. She had always taken control of things, and I was there for one reason only, and that was to find Troy. I knew Trisha would not want one second spent on her which could be spent looking for Troy.

By the time I had flown for ten hours and Judy had taken me to the hotel, I did not know what to expect. I knew Trisha would be fully focused on Troy and that all I could do was do my best to help her find him. This reunion was not about Trisha and me.

When I finally reached the hotel I nearly walked straight past Trisha. Her face was so swollen, I hardly recognised her, but something made me look back. It was Trisha. Small and bruised. Her hair was still unwashed and had mud and small bits of debris all through it.

I didn't know what to say to Trisha. What do you say to someone whose husband is missing? 'It's good to see you' seems so stupid. So I just said nothing.

As soon as Tracey arrived, it was straight down to business. Organised as ever, she had brought pictures of Troy from our wedding which she planned to use in her efforts to find him. Two men from the Australian Embassy came to meet Tracey and I, and they gave her a list of three hospitals in Bangkok which had a relationship with the embassy. They spoke to the nurses and explained that I would be going to Bangkok.

In the meantime, Tracey got going on her search. Almost as soon as she had arrived she was gone.

Before she left, she reached into her bag and pulled out her discman. 'Here, why don't you listen to this while I go and look for Troy.'

Tracey took one of the photos and left the others in her bag with me, and then took the rest to go looking through Krabi Hospital. When she was gone I reached down into her bag and pulled out the picture of Troy. It was us together exchanging vows on our wedding day. He was smiling his big smile. I slid down in my chair, placed the earphones on my head and pressed play. The walkman was cued at one of our favourite songs, 'My Happiness' by Powderfinger. I turned it up full blast, stared at the photo in my hands and bawled my eyes out.

Tracey had also left a phone with me. I called Belly. I'm not sure why, I think maybe because he knew more about Troy and I as a couple than almost anyone, and I just needed to hear from someone who wasn't my family. The thought of going back to Melbourne without Troy was too much. I could not live without him, and if he had died, then I wished the wave had killed me too. How could I ever face his friends and family? I needed to hear from Belly in person – not just a text message – that I had a reason to come home.

Belly didn't say much. He never did. Around the football club he was called 'Humphrey' because in his first year he didn't say a word. In his wedding speech, Troy was going to tell Belly that he loved him but he chickened out, so I said it in my speech instead. I said that Troy and I both loved Belly and he would have been a bridesmaid if Troy had not asked him to be a groomsman.

At about 1 pm the Canadian family who had helped me on the Viewpoint arrived to see how I was going. They had been to Krabi to look for me and had heard that I would be here. When they walked in I was amazed they had gone to so much effort to find me. I realised then that helping me had had a big effect on them, and I was glad to have the opportunity to thank them.

Tracey returned. There was still no news of Troy. The embassy had arranged a minibus and a plane to Bangkok so I could transfer to a hospital where I could get my leg seen to. On the plane there was a Canadian girl seated opposite us whose head was half wrapped in a bloody bandage. She must have been hit pretty hard because the whole side of her face was swollen over and purple. She just sat there the whole way silently crying to herself. I felt I understood what she was going through. The real pain had nothing to do with the injuries. The real pain was the guilt of leaving someone behind.

When we arrived at Bangkok airport, Tracey took out her mobile and started scrolling down the message menu. I watched her facial expressions. She listened intently and then started to make calls.

'Tracey, what is it?' I asked. 'Tracey, tell me.'

For a second Tracey looked up at me. 'I think they might have found Troy.' Despite these words being the ones I had wanted to hear for almost three days now, something in the way she spoke didn't inspire the confidence I was looking for.

'Tell me. What? Where? Is he okay?'

By this stage, Tracey was waving her hand at me to be quiet. But the more she checked her messages, the more her body slumped. It had been a false alarm. Channel 7 had reported that Troy had been found alive, but that there was still no confirmation. In the end it was discovered that my name had appeared on the 'found list' twice, once as T. Silvers (my maiden name) and once as T. Broadbridge. It was a blow, but I don't blame anyone for it.

When we reached the Bangkok Nursing Home, it was 8 pm and I was taken straight to intensive care. When I was wheeled into the operating theatre a weird thing happened. One of the doctors leaned over and said, 'We understand your pain. We have just heard that the king's grandson has been killed.' To a Thai, losing a member of the royal family is like losing a member of your own family. Once again, I momentarily saw that this tragedy was much bigger than just my own pain.

The operation was to remove the infection in my leg, as there was a real possibility I would lose my leg altogether. It was late at night when I went into the operating room – the last operation of the day – and very early in the morning when I came out. They wheeled me back into the intensive care unit and Tracey was sleeping on the couch waiting for me. I was still half drugged from the operation and my leg hurt like hell.

As I gradually came to, I realised I was busting to go to the toilet, but I could hardly move. I tried to wake Tracey by tapping my wedding ring on the railings of the hospital bed, but I was so weak I could not wake her. When the nurse finally came, I was unable to raise myself onto a bedpan and so, just when I thought things could not possibly get worse, the nurse returned with a nappy. She lifted me up and tied it around my waist. I had lost the final control. Usually this would have made me extremely self-conscious, but after what I had been through, what did it matter?

Chapter 5

29 DECEMBER 2004: *Help from Home*

The following day Mum and Emeli both arrived. I was so glad to see them both, but it was particularly good to have Emeli there. Emeli and I had met on a Reach camp at Santa Monica in Lorne about seven years before, and we had been through a lot together, including the death of both her mother and her father.

At that time in my life, and with all that we had shared, I don't think I could have had a better person by my side. At her mother's funeral, I remember watching Emeli try to hold herself together. We spoke about it later and she said how unhealthy she thought it was for people not to express their feelings during funerals. She mentioned how whenever you see a Middle Eastern funeral on television, the women howl and wail over the casket. To us it seems an overreaction, but as Emeli had known and I was now finding out, it is probably much healthier than the restraint and inner control many of us are taught to show in our society.

Emeli's story

Trisha has always been a hard person to get to know well. When I first met her at Reach, her idea of being emotional and tactile was to touch someone on the shoulder. She was always so guarded, but there was this loyalty about her that I really liked. It was kind of like, once you were her friend she was with you no matter what.

So when I heard the news about the tsunami, all I could think was that I had to go over to be with her. I arrived in Bangkok on the morning of 29 December and went straight to the hospital where Trisha had just had her operation. When I walked into the room, I could not believe this was the same girl whose wedding I had been to two weeks earlier. Her face was swollen to twice its normal size. Her left eye was purple and black and there was no gap between her nose and her cheek. For some reason I had not expected her to look so bad.

The operation on her knee had also just been completed but the wound was still open. It was like someone had attacked her with an axe and split her leg to the bone. When I arrived, Trisha was still groggy and the nurses were unpacking the gauze which had filled her knee. I have never seen a person look so vulnerable. Her swollen face looked up from a ridiculously clean white pillow, pleading with the nurses as they pulled away the gauze. 'Please stop,' she was saying. 'Please don't hurt me any more.'

It was now entering into the fourth day since Troy had disappeared and the chances of finding him alive were almost zero. When Trisha was feeling a little better, we asked her what she wanted us to do.

'I want you to go and find Troy,' she said resolutely. Looking back, I think by then even Trisha knew the search was hopeless, but we contacted the embassy and started to make a list of places we should go to look.

Tracey and I flew to Phuket to check through the hospitals and morgues. There were eight hospitals and we hoped to cover them in two days. The embassy had told us they were also searching, so we felt confident that, for better or worse, we would find Troy soon.

On arrival at Phuket airport, we were confronted with the strangest sight. The airport was packed and very hectic, but there was no real indication of where to go to look for survivors. The embassy had told us to look on noticeboards and poles where people often left information. As we got off the plane and walked through the gates, every pole in the airport area was plastered with the same poster. As we drew closer we realised all of them were of Troy in his Melbourne jumper. The embassy must have downloaded his photo from the internet. Underneath were written four simple words and a phone number: Troy Broadbridge, Missing, Call [the number].

We walked from pole to pole, each with Troy's smiling face looking down on us, but even with the footy jumper and the big smile, he might as well have been a million miles away.

Eventually we managed to get in contact with embassy officials who told us point blank that every indication pointed to the fact that Troy was dead. There did not seem to be even a shadow of doubt.

After leaving the airport, we went straight to a giant open park area which had become known as Ground Zero. The entire Thai relief program was run from here. Basically it was a kilometre of noticeboards and about two dozen tables set up with representatives from each country manning them. As we walked past the rows and rows of pictures, one thing became very clear to us. This event was bigger than anyone back home could possibly imagine.

For the next two days we went from meeting to meeting and morgue to morgue. Most of the identification was done from photos. After a while the faces seemed to blur into each other. Each time I turned a page another life clicked over, another family was sharing our pain, another child somewhere was without a parent.

We went to the Hilton Hotel where the Australian Embassy had set up an information centre. The Phuket Hilton is a phenomenal hotel, and so out of place under the circumstances. We walked into the huge lobby which was full of trimmings and waterfalls and massive marble pillars, and followed the signs to the information centre. On the way, we passed a desk set up by the embassy offering rooms for 500 baht per night (about $20), so we booked one.

When we found the embassy staff, to our amazement we were the only ones there. We were expecting it be packed full of people like us searching for friends and relatives. Not one other family! So Tracey and I walked into this grand meeting room and sat down at a table with four uniformed police, the former Australian ambassador, the current ambassador and the Australian military advisor for Thailand! They also had a chaplain, a representative from the Australian Federal Police, and a counsellor.

We were in there for about an hour asking questions, and they provided us with masses of information. All of it was bad. Searches through the beach area on Phi Phi Island where Troy and Trisha had been hit by the wave had yielded no survivors. The more the search parties dug, the greater the body count was growing. 'Even if we find the body, it will take weeks to identify,' said the ambassador. 'After the Bali bombing,' he continued, 'the first body was not confirmed for eight weeks.'

I kept trying to divert them from using the term body. But they had been through this before. Troy was dead, and even though there was no body to prove it, there was no use denying it any more.

We slept that night in the luxury of the Hilton Hotel for $20, while somewhere out there Troy's body was waiting to be found.

When Tracey and Emeli finally returned from Phuket it was New Year's Eve and Mum was waiting with me. The news from Emeli was not unexpected, but for me it was the final blow. Until that moment I had been clinging to the thought that Troy might be unconscious in a hospital somewhere, but now I realised there were too many people out looking for him, all over Thailand. There was no hope of finding Troy alive.

Meanwhile, my leg was starting to get worse again, despite a second operation, and I needed to get it seen to properly. The embassy had sent all Troy's and my luggage to the hospital, as it turned out our hotel on Phi Phi had not been destroyed, so I had my passport and all our belongings.

It was time to go home.

Chapter 6

Finding Troy

As the days wore on, I began to see how big the tsunami disaster was and how many people had been affected. It seemed every day another 10,000 people were added to the death toll. It's hard to explain, but when you talk in thousands it is easy for people to miss the full picture. I was so caught up in my own grief, I had hardly taken the time to think how this was affecting the rest of the world. The death toll was now over 200,000, but it's not until the toll goes to 200,001 and the 'one' is someone you love that the numbers begin to have real meaning.

For everything I was feeling, there were a quarter of a million families going through the same pain. All over the world people were holding out hope for survivors, feeling as powerless and vulnerable as I was. All over the world fathers and mothers like Troy's were waiting for news.

I can only imagine what it must have been like for Wayne to fly over to Thailand still holding onto the faint hope that Troy might be alive. At least I had the chance to be active in my search for

Troy right from the start, but for those at home in Australia, the wait for news must have been a hugely difficult time.

When Wayne arrived in Thailand, he spent days searching through morgues and talking to doctors and volunteers who may have treated Troy. Wayne's brother-in-law, John, had made the trip with him and between them I think they secretly hoped they would find Troy sitting up in a hospital somewhere. I suppose we were all holding onto that thin thread.

As I understand it, at that stage most of the searching for bodies was done by looking through photographs or images on the internet. Clicking through image after image must have taken its toll on Wayne, but I guess nothing in life could have prepared him, or anyone else, for the moment when Troy's body was finally identified.

It was 3 January, the day we were due to fly out of Bangkok, when I heard the news. By this time Tracey and Emeli had already returned home and Mum and I were preparing to board our flight. Mum checked her phone. There were thirty-one missed calls, mostly from Wayne. We knew the news was either very good or very bad. I dreaded what I almost certainly knew would be the message.

We called Wayne back and when we finally managed to get through, I could hardly hold the phone up to my ear to listen. As soon as I heard the tone of his voice, I knew. I can't remember the conversation. All I knew was that the love of my life was dead. It was real. I felt my life was over, and I was filled with a mix of sadness and anger.

At Singapore airport we had to transfer to our flight to Melbourne. Due to my injuries I was put into a wheelchair for transit, but it could not fit through the gates. I was so angry, 'Haven't you ever had someone come through in a wheelchair before?' I yelled.

On the plane I was placed in an aisle seat. Apart from my facial wounds and my bandaged leg, I was just another passenger flying from Singapore to Melbourne – at that point no one on board knew what had happened to me. As the flight was due to take off, a flight attendant came around with copies of the *Herald Sun*. I took one, thinking it might help to read about home, but when I saw the front page my heart froze. The entire page was filled with a picture of Troy and me from our wedding. I broke down and started sobbing, pleading with the hostess to take the papers away.

I tried everything I could to keep it together. I tried to watch a movie and listen to music, but my mind wouldn't rest. It was like my whole body was numb, but my brain kept turning things over and over. The thought of how Troy had actually died haunted me every second. Did he suffer? Was it quick? Each time I closed my eyes I saw images of his body rolling around in the water.

I was overcome by guilt that I had survived. I had no idea how I was going to face Troy's friends and family when I returned. Troy's body was lying somewhere in a morgue in Thailand and I was here in this plane. It was all so wrong.

I must have looked such a mess. The passenger next to me kindly offered to move so that I could lie down and rest my leg. Throughout the flight I sobbed silently to myself. It was too much – seeing Troy and me on the front page had plunged me into total despair. If I could have opened the door across the aisle and jumped out of that plane, I would have.

My mood varied from absolute anger to total devastation. Sometimes I wanted to scream, 'How dare you take him away from me?' I wanted to beat up the world. At other times I just wanted to end it all, to stop the constant questioning, guilt and emotional pain which haunted all my thoughts. Whenever I thought I would lose it completely, I started training myself to hold on a little longer. In that moment, Troy's voice would come to me – I'd feel his hands around me and hear him whisper to me. I knew he would say I was stronger than this. Troy was like that. All through his footy career he battled injury and disappointment and we worked through it together. Sometimes I was his strength, and now he was mine.

As we were coming in to land, a young woman about my age who must have recognised me from the newspaper leant across the aisle and tapped me on the shoulder. 'I have no idea what you are going through,' she said, 'but I have always worn this bracelet to bring me strength. I was wearing it when I survived a car accident. It means a lot to me but I want you to have it.'

I had no idea what to say, so I accepted it. It was the first of many gestures of kindness I was to receive in the months to come.

That plane flight back to Melbourne was the longest seven hours of my life. Just fourteen short days ago, Troy and I had boarded a plane for Thailand, full of love and hope and setting out on the rest of our life's journey.

Now I was returning alone.

Part Two

Before the Wave

Troy was destined to play footy. Here he is as a young boy, playing footy in Adelaide.

Right: Troy with Wayne and Pam.
Left: Big brother Troy with sisters Jayne and Sarah (right) and younger brother Sam.

In many ways my destiny was sport. Here, I'm in Year 8 at Balwyn High, playing girls' footy.

Troy, playing for Sandringham in 2000, with his troublesome shoulder strapped.

Sandringham's premiership team 2004 and Troy's last game. Troy is hiding, as usual, near the middle at the back. Luke is on the far left, kneeling; Belly is on Troy's right; Lamby is right at the back near Belly.

Back row: *Travis Johnstone, Luke Williams, Paul Newman, Dale Carson, Daniel Bell, Chris Heffernan, Simon Godfrey, Chris Johnson, Daniel Ward, Scott Thompson, Cameron Hunter, Phillip Read.* ***Third row:*** *Chris Fagan (assistant coach), Brett Ratten (assistant coach), Paul Wheatley, Troy Broadbridge, Jared Rivers, Ben Holland, Ryan Ferguson, Mark Jamar, Darren Jolly, Brad Miller, Nick Smith, Chris Lamb, Luke Molan, Nathan Carroll, Mark Riley (assistant coach), Mark Williams (Sandringham coach).* ***Second row:*** *Peter Walsh, Guy Rigoni, Brad Green, Jeff White, Russell Robertson, David Neitz (captain), Neale Daniher (coach), Adem Yze, Cameron Bruce, Clint Bizzell, Alistair Nicholson, Nathan Brown.* ***Front row:*** *Joel Campbell, Aaron Davey, Matthew Whelan, Brock McLean, Adam Fisher, Colin Sylvia, Steven Armstrong, James McDonald, Peter Vardy.*

Chapter 7

Best Friends

I first met Troy at the Bentleigh Club, the social club for the Melbourne Football Club, in 1999. We were both just starting AFL traineeships. A lot of young footballers do traineeships to help them find work in sports-related industries, but traineeships are also open to young people interested in careers such as sports administration. Sport had always been my passion, so at seventeen I'd jumped at the chance to follow my older brother Tim into a traineeship.

I was waiting to sign some documents when Troy walked in with his arm in a sling – as usual he was injured – accompanied by Melbourne's player welfare officer, Stephen Newport. Troy had been drafted onto Melbourne's rookie list from South Australia and was playing in the seconds. Most clubs keep players on the rookie list for no more than two years, so they're under a lot of pressure to train and play hard in the hope they impress the selectors and make it onto the senior list.

I remember thinking how incredibly shy Troy was. He hardly

looked at me for the whole meeting, fidgeting around and smiling nervously every now and then. I think it's fair to say the other thing I noticed about Troy was his ears. He was only eighteen, so he still looked like a kid and hadn't grown into his body yet. A lot of young AFL guys are like that: they get drafted as teenagers and it takes three or four years of weights before they fill out and can play in the senior side. Despite being really shy and awkward, Troy always had this quiet inner confidence, which is even more important than size if you want to play sport at the elite level.

Young guys in the AFL do it pretty tough, especially when they are rookie players who have come from interstate with no guarantee of making it to the seniors. I guess Troy had arrived in Melbourne with a massive weight of expectation on his shoulders and here he was, working in a hotel bar on a traineeship with a dislocated shoulder and his arm in a sling instead of playing football. It is a side of the AFL the public don't see: for every superstar there are thirty guys who are borderline, hanging onto their dream by a thin thread, battling from week to week to keep up the intensity and not let the pressure of being delisted get to them. The wage is very different from the seniors, too. When Troy was on the rookie list, his base was $18,000.

At first I felt sorry for him. We crossed paths now and then, and I would smile at him which made him go red with embarrassment. But underneath his embarrassment was the most incredible smile I have ever seen. Ask most people what they remember about Troy and they will talk about his smile. It was a privilege to have him smile at you, and pretty soon I was hooked on it and started hoping I'd bump into him just to see it.

After a few weeks I decided to ask Troy out with some friends for a few drinks. He was still injured and unable to play, so going out wasn't the big issue it became when he was in training. Looking back, it all seems backwards: I asked him out; I even picked him up that night. Troy and Luke Taylor, another Melbourne player, were boarding in Ashwood. From Ashwood, we went around to my friend's house and met up with the girls, then rocked up to Casey's Nightclub. So there was quiet little Troy, on his own with six hot eighteen-year-old girls. He never said a word, but he couldn't get the smile off his face.

When we got to the door there was a bit of a queue, and while we were waiting we all noticed a sign which said 'No Dogs Allowed'. Troy looked at us with his massive smile, and said, 'Looks like you girls are in trouble. I'll see you inside.'

We laughed our heads off. It was a side to Troy I hadn't seen, and I wondered if perhaps he wasn't so shy after all.

In the months that followed, our friendship grew slowly. Troy missed about eight weeks with his dislocated shoulder before he started back in the seconds. The thought was that he would last the season and then get a shoulder reconstruction at the end of the year.

I didn't tell Troy, but I went to watch him play. I didn't know him well then, but I knew the last thing he wanted was to go back to Adelaide branded a failure for not having made it at AFL level. Back then, seconds footy was played before the senior game, and although they were playing on the big grounds there were never many people there to watch. Most of the guys playing were either hanging on to the end of their careers or hoping to make it onto the senior list.

This was Troy's second game back. There I was at 11:30 on a Sunday morning sitting in a freezing cold, empty grandstand, watching Troy playing in the ruck and hoping he'd have a good game.

At one point he missed the ball and punched the air, which forced his shoulder to pop out again. That was it. He would have to have the shoulder reconstruction now and miss the rest of the season.

When the senior game started, Troy came up the stairs to where the players sat, his arm in a sling. He was struggling to eat a sandwich – it kept falling apart as he raised it to his mouth. I could see he was in pain from the shoulder, but he was in even more pain from the disappointment. Without saying anything, I went over and sat next to him. We hardly said a word, but from that moment on, I knew my place in life was next to Troy.

Troy's arm spent a lot of time in a sling over the years. When I went through Troy's things recently, I found six slings which he should have probably have taken back but, typically, he had forgotten. I also become an expert on shoulder injuries. One of the identifying signs when Troy's body was found was the surgical pin he had in his shoulder. Looking back, it's weird to think that the shoulder which caused Troy so much pain thoughout his football career was what finally set him apart.

The night after Troy popped his shoulder that second time, I rang Ashwood to speak to Troy. Luke answered and told me he had been admitted to hospital for an operation. I left a message for Troy and hung up.

Ten minutes later my phone rang. It was Troy. We talked for

an hour about everything except his shoulder. It was good to talk to him. He told me he was going back home to Adelaide for a while after the operation and he would call me when he got back.

I missed Troy while he was away, and I realised my feelings for him were changing into something stronger than friendship, but I had no idea how to tell him how I felt. My family had not been openly emotional or affectionate, so I struggled with that. I've never told my parents I love them, and we don't kiss and hug as a family.

I'd been a bit wild as a teenager, and I'd never felt completely accepted in my own family. Mum helps me enormously now, but while I was growing up Dad was going through some problems of his own, and I saw Mum as someone who was quite powerless. She rarely showed her emotions – I guess it was her way of coping – and even though I knew my family loved me, I wanted more than they could give at the time.

By the time I was fifteen I had already been to seven different schools, as Dad and Mum kept buying and selling various business, and worked in real estate and used cars, so we moved around a lot. After a stint in Queensland, my family moved down to Melbourne where I was sent to Deepdene Primary and then Balwyn High.

It was at high school that I started to develop some really bad habits. My best friend had very liberated parents and she was allowed to smoke and drink at home. It was a habit I fell into pretty easily. One night at a party her older brother kissed me, and that was it, I thought I was in love. I was crying out for affection, as anyone would have done at that time.

Looking back I was so naive. We went out together for two and half years, and I just put up with anything from him. Every weekend we would go and get drunk at the local pub, and every weekend he would end up in a fight and I would stick up for him. I started lying to my parents, staying out all night, drinking and trying to break as many rules as possible to fit in. It was crazy.

In the end he cheated on me, and because I trusted him and loved him – as much as a teenager can – I felt completely betrayed and I closed off.

When my sister Tracey announced she was going on exchange to the United States, I felt as if she was the only person left I could really trust and now she was deserting me. The night before she left we ate at a restaurant and then went drinking afterwards. All night I wanted to tell her how much I loved her and needed her, but I couldn't. The real me was too far beneath the surface.

The next morning I went into the shower and stuck something down my throat to make myself sick. Vomiting was really easy, I enjoyed the feeling. It was like I was getting rid of the bad stuff, hurting myself and trying to manipulate Tracey into staying at the same time.

Another time I took a big handful of pills and swallowed them. I wasn't trying to kill myself, I was trying to block the pain. And the pain wasn't that these people had left me but more that I had left myself. I felt so alone.

I was put in front of counsellors who could not relate to young people at all. The only thing that qualified them to speak to me was a piece of paper from a university. They were out of touch, unable to empathise and incapable of reaching out to me and helping me open up.

What changed things around for me was getting involved with Reach. I remember Jim Stynes coming to our school, and some of the things he said really stuck in my mind. He talked about the Hero's Journey Day that Reach runs and invited us to apply if we were interested. Ten places were on offer – you had to put in writing why you wanted to go. I really wanted to go and was so pleased when I was chosen. I got a lot out of that day, so when I found out that Reach also ran camps, I was keen to become more involved. Mum agreed to pay so I went to a Reach camp, and it seemed like a family environment I felt I'd never had. For the first time I saw an adult who seemed to understand what it was like to be young. Jim and the other facilitator, Paul, weren't up there saying, 'Don't drink, don't take drugs, don't get depressed, and tell the teacher if you get bullied.' Instead they were saying, 'We all know it goes on out there and that to different degrees all of you are involved at some level or another. So what are your choices?'

It was the first time anyone had talked to me about choice. I had grown up in a family where no one saw choices, while I kept getting into bad situations and blaming everyone but myself.

The final night of the camp we walked through the bush until we emerged on a stretch of rocks running along the coastline between Lorne and Wye River. To our left the sea was crashing in. As a kid I had always loved the sound and smell of the sea – it made me feel free. Earlier that day, I freaked Jim out by swimming out to sea until I was almost out of sight. I had always been a good swimmer, and I can't describe the feeling of freedom I got from being in the ocean.

Since the tsunami, I've only swum once, in a pool. I struggle to drive along Beach Road, and being in a boat completely freaks me out. But my relationship with the water is extremely strong – I have a mermaid tattoo on my back – and I know I will conquer my fear and regain that connection soon.

When we reached our destination on the walk, the Reach leaders blindfolded us and sat us down on the rocks. It was dark but we could all hear the waves. I was paired up with Jim's sister Sharon as my mentor, and I doubt I will ever meet a kinder, more loving person. She led me into a cave and sat me down and I took off my blindfold.

It was like magic. The Reach crew had filled the cave with tealight candles and there were little lights everywhere. From the back of the cave a Sarah McLachlan song was playing, and we were all sitting in a circle in front of a little fire with Jim out the front. To this day I can't explain why, but I felt really safe. I trusted the people I was with. It was the first time I felt that the spirit inside me who was Trisha was not squashed, not covered – she was there and no longer needed to hide. I was in a new environment and I didn't have to live up to anything. I was just me, and no one had any preconceived thoughts about how I should act.

Each person told a little bit of their own story. I was scared, but when it was my turn, I found myself talking about the weirdest thing. I started to talk about swimming and how I loved the sea. At the time I was training to do triathlons, and as I spoke I felt myself relaxing, I had never spoken so honestly before. It was probably the first time I managed to experience the real me, guilt-free, free from the anxiety and self-loathing which many young girls put themselves through.

Jim's memory of Trisha at the Reach camp

My main memory of Trisha on that first camp was of a lost little girl. Like so many teenagers, you could see Trisha was desperate for a place to feel safe and be able to express herself openly. When she first arrived at Reach, Trisha had a really tough exterior. You only had to look at her the wrong way and she would fire up. But on the walk home from the cave that night I saw another side of her. She talked openly and freely about her past and about the problems she had in relating to her parents and how alone she felt in the world.

Trisha was a beautiful kid with a gorgeous smile, and her positive energy was infectious. However deep down she was troubled by a heavy darkness she struggled to express. When I spoke to her very concerned mum it was difficult to understand why such a positive girl was questioning the point of life in such a negative way. She struggled to connect in a meaningful way with her family and friends and her relationship with her dad in her mind was non-existent. Yet in many ways she craved that male connection, and at first she attracted some people to her who weren't a great influence. They were mainly the rebels and they offered her some real adventure, but as she became more involved in Reach and started to look seriously at taking control of her life, she moved away from these more negative influences and started to socialise with more positive people.

In the years that followed I watched as her relationship with Troy grew stronger and together they mentored each other into adulthood. They were great together. Trisha grew from this little lost girl into a confident woman. With Troy at the centre of her life, she had a purpose; she felt she was worth something.

When Troy returned to Melbourne, we began spending a lot of time together. I was sort of seeing someone else at the time, and I was still unsure how Troy felt about me, but because of the way I was brought up I found it really hard to talk to Troy about it. I was outwardly confident but on the inside I was a mess. Troy was so quiet and restrained, it was hard to know what he was thinking and feeling.

Going back to Adelaide had been hard for Troy. He'd left to come to Melbourne with such high hopes, and had returned having played only a handful of games and spent most of the year injured. Once again I watched as he worked his way through his injury and gradually grew in confidence.

By November 1999 we were inseperable best friends. I was still at home with Mum and Dad, and Troy was practically living at our place. My parents loved having him there because he was a steadying influence on me. We watched videos and snuggled on the couch and fall asleep – nothing romantic, just enjoying each other's company. Troy was unlike any male I'd ever met. He was a gentleman and would never pressure a girl, but by this stage I was hoping he would give me some sign that he was keen.

I cared so much for Troy, and for me this was an overwhelming feeling. Finally I felt that I could be totally honest with someone and share my fears. For the first time I was starting to feel that I could really love someone. I think Troy also felt accepted by me for just being himself, that he didn't have to be someone he wasn't, which he had sometimes felt at the beginning of his time at Melbourne when he was trying to measure up and fit in.

So here we were, two individuals from different necks of the woods, thrown together – the unlikely couple – and falling in love with each other but both unable to express it.

I was the first one to crack.

On Australia Day 2000, I couldn't wait any longer. Troy picked me up to take me to the airport because I was flying around Australia to celebrate Australia Day with some kids from Reach. From attending that first Reach camp at fifteen, I had worked my way up as a group leader and later graduated as a fully-fledged Reach facilitator.

Just as we neared the airport, I couldn't hold it in any more. Admittedly I was only eighteen, but I felt about fourteen, I was so nervous. All along I had made the moves with Troy, and now I was doing it again.

'Troy, I need to tell you something.'

He looked at me like it was just another comment.

'I like you more than a friend,' I said.

Even as I said it, I was cringing. More than a friend! I sounded like a primary school kid.

To my horror, Troy didn't say a word. He just froze. There was an awful silence and he seriously did not say a word.

I had timed my declaration just as we were arriving at the airport, and when I got out of the car I was so upset, I didn't give him a chance to say anything and I just stormed off.

I got onto that plane and bawled my eyes out.

When I came home to Melbourne, I swore off men for life ... until the next day when Troy came over. We went into the kitchen. He looked at me and smiled. That was enough.

I walked right up close to him and kissed him. We both laughed – it was Troy's way of saying he felt the same.

That afternoon we went for a walk, stopping every few steps along the way to kiss like a couple of little kids. Is there anything better in life than new love?

Chapter 8

Tough Times

We didn't tell anyone for ages that we were together. I had finished my AFL traineeship and was now working at Melbourne Football Club as an events assistant, while Troy was playing for Sandringham and training hard to make it onto the senior list. We were both spending a lot of time at the club and wanted to keep things professional at work, plus I think Troy didn't want people making a big deal of our relationship while it was still so new.

Troy's football career wasn't going well at all in early 2000. His confidence was so low, at one stage he was even dropped to the Sandringham seconds. I think this was the lowest he had been in his life, and he felt he had let everyone down, including himself. But Troy ended up playing an amazing second half of the season in 2000 for Sandy seniors. Sandringham went on to win the VFL premiership that year and Troy was named one of the best players in the side. In Round 20 he was even named on the Melbourne senior list (though he didn't actually play) in place of his good friend Luke Ottens. Unfortunately Luke had been placed on the long-term injury list.

Troy was still on his low wage and driving an old Falcon which was so unreliable and always breaking down. We had very little money coming in between us to even think about moving into a place of our own. Troy was also concerned about how his parents, who were strong Catholics, would feel about us living together. I think all Troy's life his first priority had been to please his parents, and while his background had helped him develop his strong character and great sense of justice, he also felt the pressure to perform. Now he was thinking about breaking free and making a life for himself in Victoria.

When Troy signed a two-year contract with Melbourne for 2001–2002, we finally felt secure enough to rent a little one-bedroom flat in Carnegie together. It was a humble beginning to our big dream of one day buying a place of our own.

With Troy's support, in 2001 I left work at the Melbourne Football Club and went back to school to complete my VCE as a mature age student. I was studying and working for Reach as a facilitator and training development manager. It was hard, but I had a huge sense of achievement when I successfully completed the year, and Troy was so proud of me.

Another highlight of 2001 came when Troy was selected to play his first senior game for Melbourne. Troy and I drove to the game together and arrived early. I kissed him and wished him good luck and watched him walk off to the rooms. About a minute later I saw him come back and ask someone for directions. Here he was heading into his first game and he didn't even know how to get into the ground!

I sat up in the stand with a few of our friends. Troy didn't get his chance until halfway through the third quarter, but the minute he ran on, I started to cry. For the fans and maybe for the other players, it was just one of a million interchanges which happen in the AFL every year, but for me it was enormous.

Seconds later the ball came out of the centre and Troy marked it on the half-forward line. He was awarded a fifty-metre penalty which bought him right up in front of the goalposts. His first kick in AFL was a goal! I looked up on the scoreboard at the MCG and there was a huge picture of Troy with that massive smile on his face. Underneath it read: Troy Broadbridge – Games: 1, Marks: 1, Kicks: 1, Goals: 1.

Melbourne player Andrew Leoncelli, who was sitting in the stand injured that day, later told Troy that watching me at that moment was the first time he had ever seen someone laugh, cry, scream and be silent all at the same time.

Troy played nine senior games that season.

The following year, 2002, he played a further fourteen games in the seniors and was starting to make a real name for himself. I was studying Arts at Latrobe University and working part-time as a Reach facilitator, and we had moved into a flat in Balwyn that was above and behind a shop called Kluckee.

Then came Round 18, Melbourne vs Richmond at the MCG. I knew Troy had been having problems with his knee, and I was so worried about it all day. I even said to a friend before the game started, 'Troy is going to injure his knee today.' If he'd had the luxury of being a permanent senior player, he would not have played, but as someone who was still trying to consolidate his place on the team, he could not afford to miss a game.

Troy dislocated his kneecap and was stretchered off. As it was replayed on the screen, I burst into tears. I could not watch my beautiful boy be in pain; he was heartbroken. My phone rang five minutes later and it was Troy, asking me to come down to the rooms. I walked into the room and Jim was there as well – he told me to try to keep Troy positive. I looked into Troy's eyes, his sad blue eyes, and told him we could get through this. It was not over yet, and we would not let it be over.

That night dragged for what felt like a month. I got Troy home by putting down the seats of my car and lying him across the back. There were numerous phone calls from Troy's parents, my parents and Danny Corcoran, Melbourne's football manager. Danny promised us that Melbourne would re-sign Troy for 2003–2004, no matter what the result of the tests were the next day. Everyone was worried that Troy needed a knee reconstruction.

That night there was no way I could get Troy up to our bedroom, so I pulled a mattress down the stairs and put it in the lounge room for Troy to sleep on. He didn't sleep much, he was in so much pain. I kissed his cheek and held his hand all night.

I started to plan in my head what I needed to do. It was going to be a long couple of months, as Troy could not drive, go up stairs, work or play football. He would need a lot of emotional support as a serious injury would mean his career had stalled again. I called Emeli the next morning and she helped me organise for the majority of my Reach commitments to be taken over by other facilitators. With Troy unable to play, his match payments would stop, placing a huge strain on our finances, but we were masters at living on no money.

Troy went into hospital for a knee arthroscope. The worst pain was when they drained his knee. I cried and stayed with him every day until they kicked me out. I brought Troy a Beanie Kid, as a hint that I had bought him a bean bag for when he returned home from hospital.

Troy spent the rest of 2002 doing rehab and hanging around the club. It was a very frustrating time for both of us. The one bright spark was that, with the security of a new contract for 2003–2004, Troy was able to buy a house for us in Cheltenham in late 2002. His rehab had been going well and by then he was ready to play again.

Troy came back from his knee injury and played a half for the Sandringham seconds in the 2003 pre-season. I have never seen him so happy. I took photos of him on the way to the game, and after the first half he came and sat with me instead of on the bench, and cuddled me.

Unfortunately for Troy, injuries were part of the package for most of his football career. The next week Troy played for Sandringham in the seniors, and just before quarter time, he popped out his shoulder. I was talking with Chris Lamb's girlfriend, Lucy, at the time, and did not see the moment when it happened. My phone rang at quarter time – it was Troy. 'Where are you sitting?' he said. I was confused. Wasn't Troy playing? As I looked up my heart sank. Troy was walking towards me, head down, ice pack on his shoulder. I started to cry – I did a lot of that at the football – and ran to him.

'What happened?' I asked, and then all I could think to say was, 'I love you.'

I helped Troy get changed and he picked up his lunch pack. I fed him his yoghurt as we sat in the stands at Sandringham.

Troy was out for six weeks with a dislocated shoulder. He came back the same week as Alistair Nicholson, playing for Sandringham seconds at Box Hill. This write-up about it made me proud.

> *For key Melbourne defenders Alistair Nicholson and Troy Broadbridge the wait is finally over. This weekend they will make their return to football through Melbourne's VFL side Sandringham, after both suffered serious knee injuries last year ...*
>
> *When 22-year-old Troy Broadbridge went down on his knee against Richmond last year, he thought his dose of bad luck was all but behind him. However in his first comeback game with Sandringham this year, the tall defender dislocated his shoulder, requiring treatment similar to that of Shane Warne. Broadbridge explains the feeling as 'hopelessness – you just want to be out there helping the blokes. As a player sitting up in the stand each week, you see the play unfold, and know exactly what you could be doing'.*
>
> *Broadbridge's rehabilitation process was much the same as that of Steven Febey, a player hampered by shoulder problems towards the latter part of his career. 'I've had to do a great deal of physio … But I've done all the work, my knee is fine, and my shoulder feels great also. I am primed to go,' he says.*
>
> *Broadbridge's shoulder problem didn't affect his fitness and therefore he believes this year he is a much fitter and stronger*

player. During his lay-off he chose to focus much of his attention on his Physical Education / Teaching degree at university.

Clint Stanaway, demons.com.au

After all the rehabilitation I'd seen, by the fourth quarter I could see Troy was in pain on the field, swinging his arm around. 'He has to come off,' I said. And before we knew it, in the next contest Troy's shoulder popped out again, and that was it.

I ran to the rooms and did not care that I was not supposed to go in there. I saw the tears, I knew what he thought. We went into the medical room, and after forty minutes they finally got his shoulder back in place. During this time many of the players had come in to see Troy. Alistair Nicholson hopped on the phone to the Melbourne Football Club doctor, Andrew Daff. They kept giving Troy painkillers, but he just kept repeating that it was over, that was it, I would have to get a full-time job and give up study, he had let me down.

Troy never let me down. The fact that he stayed in there with his career, trying again and again, giving it everything he could, was something I always admired. I think about it heaps now. When all seems lost, I can't give up what Troy taught me, to keep on going. He taught it to me well.

Troy had a full shoulder reconstruction and spent the rest of 2003 in rehab and training. He spent a lot of time at his beloved Sandringham, helping Graeme Yeats, the coach at the time, in the coaching box, and watching Melbourne play in the finals.

Once again without Troy's match payments our finances were stretched, particularly with the new house. Troy managed to cover the mortgage, but there was no money left over. I needed to find a job with more hours and regular pay to cover all our living expenses.

In November 2003 I started working for the Western Bulldogs four days a week as their community development officer. I enjoyed the work. A lot of it involved player appearances, and you had to be a strong woman to do the job. For me, it felt like a turning point in my career: I could stand up in front of the players and not be fazed and they would respect me. It was demanding, though, because the players could call me anytime: in the evenings, on the weekends, during classes (I was still studying at Latrobe on my one day off).

It was a tough year. Troy was often down about his career, and while many of his friends were earning good money, he could not even afford to go out for lunch after training. He never bought anything for himself. If he ever did have any spare money he would only spend it on me, so I ended up buying all his clothes for him, hoping he'd like them.

We both knew that Troy was reliant on me if his footy career didn't work out, and even though he didn't like thinking he might not always be the main breadwinner of the family, he appreciated the work and study I was doing to help set us up for the future. If his career had ended, we had a couple of plans in place. We trusted each other, that was the most important thing. I was ready to do anything I could to support him financially and emotionally.

Chapter 9

Me and Troy

Being the partner of an AFL player can be hard work. Everything is about football! Many of my friends did not understand why I was no longer available to go out partying with them all the time once I started seeing Troy, but it just became impossible to live a 'normal' life of nine-to-five work with free weekends.

Troy had a very strict routine because of his training and game schedule, so my life inevitably began to work around it as well. When he was in training he was careful with his diet and would not drink any alcohol at all. Troy and I probably only had a big night out together maybe ten times in six years. He was often up at 5 am and in bed by 8:30 pm, so we rarely went out during the week. If it was something special like a twenty-first, we would go, but we would leave by 10 pm. Troy was particularly disciplined, as he was determined to give himself the very best shot at a successful career, so it was a dramatic change for me. Emeli used to say there was no use calling our place after 9 pm because no one would answer.

Weekends were taken up with football. When Troy was playing for Sandringham, he would often go and watch the Melbourne match as well, and vice versa. I've lost count of the times I sat on my own in the stand and recorded Troy's stats. The game would take up a whole day as there were regularly functions after the match to attend – celebrations, milestone games and birthdays – so we were virtually living with the team twelve hours a day, seven days a week.

Very few players get the chance to socialise outside the club environment, and Troy didn't have a lot of friends outside football because he'd come from interstate and was so quiet that it took him a long time to get to know people. Sometimes I attended non-football social functions on my own, but I hated it, so we tried to do everything together as much as possible. Once we moved into our own house in Cheltenham we became a bit more social because we had enough room to have people over.

The few times you get to spend alone with your partner are precious, and Troy always made the best of them. On my twenty-second birthday, Troy and I drove down to Geelong to watch Melbourne play. At three-quarter time, Troy pulled out a chocolate cake and lit candles and sang 'Happy Birthday' to me in the stand, with all the players' friends, families and partners around. For Troy to do that showed that he just did not care who knew how much he loved me. He knew the ribbing he'd get from his team-mates, but that never stopped him making me feel special. He loved me.

While Troy was a really sensitive person off the field, he was hard and aggressive on it. I think that's why he was such a beautiful man – he got rid of all his aggression on the field. It's also why he struggled when he was injured, as he had no physical outlet for all that frustration. It's difficult for people who don't know footballers to see how they can be two different people – and there were moments when Troy put on his 'game face' at home, which meant that he was one hundred per cent focused on what he was doing, to the exclusion of everything else.

Troy always did all the cooking. He had to learn how, because his mum had cooked for the family when he lived at home, but he liked to be in control of what he was eating. He had to eat a lot because he was so skinny and needed to gain weight so he could get stronger. I'd eat whatever he cooked, and I went from being a size eight or ten to being a size twelve from eating so much pasta.

I did try to cook one meal for Troy, in 2002. It was a roast, and I was on the phone to Mum the whole time, and it was a disaster. Troy was so kind – he insisted there was something wrong with the oven! So Troy ended up being the cook, and I looked after him in other ways.

Troy always made time to walk the dogs each day, and I loved walking with him. He would speak to anyone in the street, which he said was because of growing up in Adelaide which was more of a community than Melbourne. He could not walk past someone in the neighbourhood without saying, 'G'day.' When he walked past the park he would often speak to the young boys there, encouraging their football skills with, 'Good hands, boys.' I know he would have made a great father.

One of things I found hardest to get used to as a footballer's partner was the constant uncertainty. You have to be flexible in your expectations, or it just won't work. This is even more the case when your partner is a fringe player. From week to week, we never knew if Troy was playing for Sandringham or Melbourne, on Saturday or Sunday, so it was impossible to commit to doing anything else on weekends. Troy had to keep himself available, and sometimes in the early days we would not find out whether he was playing for Melbourne until we saw the *Footy Show* on Thursday nights! Thursday nights were nerve-racking – the club didn't call if you weren't in the team, only if you were. From week to week, we never knew how much money Troy might bring in from match payments. We used to make lists of things we needed and had to wait until he got a senior game before we could afford them. From year to year we could never even be sure he would have a job. Everything revolved around football, and for a person like me who had been independent and a bit of a feminist at heart, I found it very challenging to give my life over to someone else's.

But right from the start I had made the decision to become really involved in Troy's career. When Troy was playing well with Sandringham, I was excited for him each week prior to senior selection, and then felt his pain if he wasn't picked. When he was playing for Melbourne and they lost, we all felt the disappointment, but when they won, it was great for the rest of the week. Likewise, when my boy was playing for the seniors and doing well, I was ecstatic. I used to get so nervous before games I'd almost be sick. During the games I was in tears half the time, my heart was so in it. I was so proud of Troy, and his career and success became everything to me. In many ways watching Troy also helped me to get the best out of myself. It drove me to crave success and helped to make Troy and me a powerful team.

It may sound as though the life of a footballer's partner is all about sacrifice, but there is no doubt I gained more than I gave up. Being Troy's partner made me part of a family, the Melbourne Football Club family. A footy club is a place where everyone is striving for the same thing, and I was constantly inspired by Troy and his team-mates as they tried to live their dreams. As time wore on in my relationship with Troy, I began to care what happened to all his team-mates as well.

Footy is a cut-throat game, and every year ten or twelve players are delisted or retired and ten or twelve new ones come in. When they are delisted, most players are devastated. For many, football was their big shot at life, the only thing they ever dreamed of. They train twice a day for ten months a year and experience a massive range of highs and lows. Usually they are delisted not because they don't work as hard as everyone else, but because they are not quite skilled enough, or not the right size, or the club has too many other players like them. Every year at the best and fairest presentation I would be in tears as one or another of our friends was farewelled. Mostly those farewelled were not senior players on big money but guys who were on the edge, just making ends meet.

Football mates are different to any other mates, because even though you spend so much time together, sometimes whether or not you get a game yourself depends on one of your best friends being dropped. There was a time for Troy when the whole back line was full of his friends, but that's where he desperately wanted to be playing. One of them had to stuff up before he could get a game. To survive in AFL you have to want to get selected ahead of your mates, you have to prove to the coach that you should play and not someone else, so it can give an edge to the friendship. Players have told me that the way Troy supported other players' careers was rare and a real standout in a cut-throat world. Troy tried very hard to accept that there was always a reason for who was selected, and that above all it was about putting together a team that would work well together on the field.

Overseas footy trips can be a great way for the team to let off steam at the end of the season and hang out as friends, without the stress and competition of selection, away from the attention of the media. Troy was not a huge fan of footy trips, but in 2002 we found the money to send him to Bali with the team. Troy had missed half the season with his knee injury, so he was looking forward to time with the boys.

There is an old saying that what goes on the footy trip stays on the footy trip, but Troy's trip to Bali would be remembered for all the wrong reasons.

Luke Williams describes the trip to Bali

Footy trips had grown to legendary status in 1980s, and as always, the Melbourne Football Club trip left the day after the best and fairest award was announced. Not surprisingly, given he had kicked eighty-two goals and gained all-Australian selection that year, David Neitz won the award and a few of the boys helped him party on into the night.

The next morning at the airport is always a classic. The boys rock up in various states of health, but as usual Troy had gone home early with Trisha so he was looking all right and was a little more prepared for the trip than some of the other boys!

The plane left at six that morning and despite a heavy night, a few of the boys got into it early. We work so hard during the year that there is nothing like a footy trip to let off steam.

When we arrived in Bali, we were booked into the Hard Rock Cafe in Kuta and prepared for a solid week ahead. Every night we went to the Sari Club along with members of the Sandringham, Geelong and Fremantle football clubs, and every night the place was packed. There was a smattering of other AFL players there in town who had been seen around, including Micky Martyn and Jason McCartney. Broady was one of the quieter ones in the group and was the first home most nights of the trip.

On our last evening, we were due to leave from the airport at 11 pm, so we had a final team dinner before climbing on board our team bus about 9 pm to head back to the airport. A few of the boys had arranged to stay on in Bali – our teammates Steve Febey, Dave Robbins and Steven Armstrong.

Finally we reached the airport and unloaded into the terminal. As we were checking in suddenly all the lights went off at the airport, then came on again ten seconds later. I was standing around with Troy and a few other guys, getting ready to board our plane, when David Schwarz received a phone call on his mobile from Steven Febey to say a bomb had exploded in Paddy's Bar and then another had gone off in the Sari Club and that it was bad. The first thing I thought was that the Melbourne guys we left behind were all there, as well as some of my friends from Sandringham.

At that stage it was too late to go back, and our football manager Danny Corcoran made the right decision to get us all on that flight and out of there. The plane trip home was horrible. What had started out as a fun time ended in disaster. For some reason, we started trying to make a list of people that we knew would be at the bar that night. On the basis of the phone call from Steve Febey, it seemed unlikely those in the Sari Club had survived. We tried to support each other but we were all consumed by the consequences of what had happened.

The flight home was eight hours. Thankfully on arrival we discovered that the bombing was bad, but all of those we knew were alive – though most had suffered injuries on varying scales.

I think the Bali bombing was kind of a wake up call to Australia. It made us all feel vulnerable, as if even here in Australia we could be touched.

The Bali bombing on 12 October 2002 was horrendous and shocking on so many levels. The whole time Troy was in the air we didn't know who had been hurt or even killed. The AFL community can be close-knit at times, so the news that Kangaroos footballers Jason McCartney and Mick Martyn had been seriously injured, and that others from the WA league had been killed, was devastating. I felt I needed to put my feelings into words for Troy, so I wrote him a letter.

The Bali bombing has affected me in a way that I am trying to suppress. Troy, I keep thinking about those people who lost loved ones, and knowing that it could have been me makes me feel sick.

> *Troy, in the instant that I heard the news, I knew in that moment how much I couldn't live without you. There would be no point. You are everything to me. Without you, I would be lost. I would be in so much pain, losing you would mean losing everything.*

> *Troy, I have never been so appreciative of the relationship we have until this week. I feel lucky and I feel I should never take for granted the fact that we are together and I have you here by my side.*

The events in Bali brought home to me how short life could be and how senseless some of the fights between Troy and I had been.

In the lead up to Christmas 2001, Troy's parents had asked him to come home to Adelaide and spend Christmas with them. We'd had an argument about it, and I was feeling very frustrated. I had to drop something off for Reach so I'd left without resolving things, but I did not think it was on really bad terms or anything.

When I returned, Troy had gone. I rang his mobile and there was no answer. It was then I knew that he was driving to Adelaide, as he had always said he would if there was no more 'us', because he would have no reason to stay. I realised I had behaved irrationally like women tend to do, and I just wanted to hold him and apologise.

I don't think I even locked the door as I ran out that day. I got straight into the car and headed west. I am not proud of the way I drove, but I kept telling myself that the faster I went, the more chance I had of catching him. Each time I saw a Falcon ahead I sped up, hoping it would be Troy.

By the time I got to Bordertown, I had been driving for six straight hours and I didn't even know if I had enough money for petrol to make it to Adelaide. Then I saw his car. I was so relieved to read the number plates, and I pulled up right next to it.

In the window of the diner, there was Troy eating a bucket of chips. I stood at the window and stared until he looked up. He saw me and came running out. We were both crying, holding each other. It was pretty symbolic when you look back on it: there we were, together, halfway between his family and mine, in the middle of nowhere with nothing really but each other. I found out later he'd left because he thought I had left him. Basically it was a massive misunderstanding, but it changed our relationship dramatically. We both knew we were not going to leave each other again. No more secrets, no more 'you and me', it was 'we'.

From then on Troy and I had our ups and downs, but it became clear to me that I did not ever want to live my life without him. It had taken us a while to get things right, but when we did, I knew that all the difficult times had bought us closer together.

In 2003, Troy wrote me a letter that showed he felt the same way.

Dear Trisha,

This is a letter that I want you to keep forever. It will hopefully remind you of why we are as we are, one entity. Trisha Silvers, you mean the world to me. You are my whole world. I love waking up in your bed, knowing that you are there. You make me feel secure, knowing that I can bounce all my stupid, crazy, out-there ideas off you and you will come up with the correct solution.

When you stay together for a long, long time there are things that are a given. There are going to be good days and there are going to be bad days. There are going to be some exciting days and there are going to be heaps and heaps of boring, unexciting, uneventful days. And it is in these boring days that you truly find out who you are supposed to be with in life. If you are still truly happy watching nothing on TV together, or eating the same spag bog for the thousandth time together, then it's supposed to be. The same can be said if you do these things and they feel like time wasting when you are not together. I even love it when you are angry with me, because then at least I know you are thinking about me. I love all the time we are together, all of it. Even writing this now reminds me of not being with you.

My life would not work without you here. I cannot imagine where I would be if you did not share this house or this life with me. I have to have you in my life. If we were not to stay together then my life would lose all of its reason. I would battle to live. It would be tough to face each lonely day.

The greatest thing that we have going for us is that underneath the relationship we are the best of friends. The friendship that we have will always get us through the no-good days. We enjoy our own company. I can only truly open up to you because you are the only one I trust.

I will love to marry you and one day I will ask you. There is no time limit or due date on marriage. We will be happy living together, married or unmarried. The ring doesn't bring with it eternal happiness. The days before and the days after the wedding will still be twenty-four hours long, some good, some not so good.

I see that we have a very stable, loving, friendly, caring relationship that allows us both to enjoy one another as well as excel at our chosen professions. We are both very driven and achievers, meaning that we both strive for our goals. The only way we can keep achieving is with the support of each other. Having said that I believe that you would still achieve without me, but I would obviously struggle without you.

I really want to be a dad and have some kids roaming around the house. But I couldn't stand it if I was an average dad. I really want to be a wise man who is respected by his kids as a loving father (there aren't too many of these around). I want the kids to still be happy to see and play with me when they are toddlers, adolescents and adults.

Here is my life timeline:

Birth	*5 October 1980*
Drafted MFC	*March 1999*
Bust Shoulder	*April 1999*
Meet Trisha	*May 1999*
Love Trisha	*June 1999*

Kiss Trisha	*27 January 2000*
Live with Trisha	
Move to Carnegie	
Play first game MFC	*June 2001*
Move to Balwyn	
Bust knee	*July 2002*
Buy House	*November 2002*
Go to Fiji	*December 2002*
Bust shoulder	*April 2003*
Propose	*when appropriate*
Marry	*6 months to a year after proposal*
(Trisha Broadbridge sounds good)	
Kid No. 1	*Madi – nine months after marriage*
Move to Perth	*Post football*
Kid No. 2	*Milla*
Kid No. 3	*Jack*
Kid No. 4	*Jerry*
Buy van to drive kids to school	
Fifth wedding anniversary in Cook Islands	

Nothing in my life has been structured so I can't really structure anything beyond what has already happened. There are events that will take place and I just hope that your timeline is exactly the same as mine.

Trisha
I truly love you and only you
I know that we will live a long and loving life together

Please stand by me
I will stand by you
Always

Love you skipper,

Love Troy
(2003)

Chapter 10

Will You Be My Wife?

In early 2004 Troy's grandfather became very ill and sadly passed away. I did not go with Troy to the funeral, but it obviously affected him strongly as he rang me from the airport the night of his return and asked me to wait up for him.

When he got home, I was working on an essay that was due and my mind was engrossed in it, so I wasn't really prepared for what was about to happen. Troy came in and told me he wanted to talk to me in the bedroom. We got into bed and he started to read from a little black notebook he had bought and written in while over in South Australia.

Dear Trisha,

I have learned a lot from this recent trip. While standing at Pop's funeral, I realised life passes you by and you get old really quick. There is so much that I need to cram into my life. I could even feel myself getting old as I stood at the funeral. I said to myself, 'It's time to take the next step with Trisha. I want a wife, I want kids, I want a house full of love and happiness.'

It is time for me to grow up. I know you will bring me happiness. I want to feel those warm fuzzy feeling I get when I look at you. I want the love and security you give me. You help me feel life.

I want to remember you as the eighteen-year-old carefree girl I first met at the Bentleigh Club and yet still hold you as the beautiful woman you have become. I want to be with you when you are thirty-five, a stunning and wonderful mother. I want to hold you when you are sixty and walk by your side as we watch our grandchildren play. I am excited and privileged at the chance I have before me.

As he continued to read, I still wasn't sure where this was leading, but my heart was bursting.

I used to think marriage would not really change our relationship, but now I see things differently. Marriage is a bond of pure strength. A bond which means everything we do, we do together. A bond which means I have to stand up and do what is right for me and my family.

I have always used footy as an excuse for putting things off. But being here at this funeral, I can see now that it is the footy which comes and goes, and you that I need.

Troy paused and put down the notebook. He took my hand and looked me straight in the eye. 'Will you be my wife?'

As he had just been reading from his notebook I was unsure whether he was actually asking me to marry him or not. So when he finished I didn't say anything.

There was a pause and then he looked at me and asked again, 'Will you be my wife?'

This time I did not hesitate, and said, 'Yes.'

By now it was very early the next morning, and we sat in bed together discussing when we wanted to get married. This October was too soon, but Troy did not want to wait until the following October, which was the long end of season football break. With my uni commitments as well, we decided to make it December 2004, when the boys usually got a ten-day break that would allow us to go on a short honeymoon.

At 8 am that morning we were at my parents' house. Troy was great. He walked into the lounge room where my father was reading the paper and asked him for my hand in marriage. Dad just looked at Troy and asked one simple question. 'Do you love her?'

Troy, of course, said, 'Yes.'

We had an engagement party two weeks later on Easter Sunday at the Reach Dream Factory. We were unsure whether Troy would be playing for Sandringham or Melbourne so this was the only day we could be sure he would be free. In the end Troy played for Sandy in Tasmania on the Saturday and returned that night. We invited the Melbourne team, the Reach crew, and our family and friends. We knew we were not going to have a big wedding so we invited all our friends to enjoy this celebration. Troy's family drove from Adelaide that day.

Jim put together a slide show of photos of us, to the accompaniment of a *Grease* song. My bridesmaids Emeli and Kirsten sang our favourite song, 'My Happiness' by Powderfinger – the same song that my sister Tracey would later hand me in Thailand. These days I find it hard to listen to, as unlike in the song, I know that Troy will not be coming back.

Josh Schmidt stole the spotlight with his sole interpretative dance to 'I Was Made For Loving You' by KISS, which led to it being the theme song for our wedding. I look back at the photos of the engagement party and I am so grateful so many of our friends got to experience that night with us – everyone was so happy for us and said we made a great team.

Troy asked Chris Lamb to be his best man, and Daniel Bell and Luke Williams to be groomsmen, along with his brother Sam. Chris had been drafted the same year as Troy and was his closest friend at the footy club.

As the 2004 season drew to a close, it became clear that Chris would be delisted at the end of the year. Troy had had a great year and played probably his best game ever for Melbourne in the elimination final which they lost to Essendon, but while a lot of his team-mates started their holidays, Troy stuck by his best mates who were enjoying success with Sandringham and still playing in the finals. He was motivated by the thought of playing in a VFL grand final with his three best mates – Chris, Daniel and Luke. Troy had played enough games in the reserves to qualify for the VFL finals, but the rules stated that only twelve AFL-listed players could play. While Troy was reluctant to take the spot of one of his mates – especially since they'd played more games for Sandy than him that year – he was still eager to be part of the grand final team. Troy was told he would not play unless there was an injury, but he still wanted to train and be part of the finals campaign even if it meant sitting in the coach's box.

On the morning of the grand final our home phone rang and it was the Sandringham coach, Mark Williams. Troy was in the shower. I rushed to get him, crying even before he got on the phone. Troy hung up and said he had to pack his footy bag, and quickly called the Sandy captain, Chad Liddell, for a lift to the game. I looked Troy in the eye that morning and said, 'Are you sure you should play?' Troy had not had the ideal preparation for the game because he hadn't thought he'd be playing, but Nick Smith was sick and couldn't play. I worried about Troy's injuries and that he wouldn't perform at his best – he'd had a full-on weekend attending a workshop and had gone out the night before for a couple of beers.

Troy just said, 'I have to play with Lamby.' And he did, with Chris securing the premiership by taking a mark on the goal line to prevent a Port Melbourne goal.

I went onto the oval after the win and watched Troy, Chris, Luke and Belly accept their premiership medals, feeling so much pride that I cried again. Troy gave me the biggest hug that day, and as I went to walk back to the stands he said, 'You're coming with me.' He took me down into the rooms and proudly told a couple of Sandy players that I was his fiancée.

After the club song had been sung, I went and sat with Troy where he chatted proudly to one of his team-mates about our upcoming wedding. He had nothing to worry about that day. He knew he had proven himself to be good enough for the senior list and would be offered a contract for 2005–2006. Troy was just so happy – he had played footy with his best mates, they had won a premiership (which is what footy is all about!) and he was now going to focus on marrying the woman he loved.

Troy knew he had played his last game with Lamby, but little did he know it would be his last game ever. I look back on that now and think how amazing his two last games were: finals footy for Melbourne, and a premiership with Sandy. I am so proud that his final football games were two of his best ever.

River boarding was part of our action-packed holiday in New Zealand, Christmas 2003.

Off the field: the funny side of quiet Troy that not everyone saw.

With my bridesmaids: from left, Emeli Paulo, Carly Schmidt, Tracey Silvers and Kirsten Emes.

Troy with his groomsmen: from left, Chris Lamb, Daniel Bell, Sam Broadbridge and Luke Williams.

During the minute's silence for Troy at the tribute match. From right, David Neitz, Adem Yze and Guy Rigoni.

Chapter 11

The Big Day

The next few months flew by as the day of our wedding approached.

My hunt for a wedding dress lasted about one hour. Mum saw a dress in Camberwell at a shop called Mimma Priolo and called me to come down and have a look. I tried it on and loved it. We looked around a bit after that, but I had already made up my mind, and that was the dress I wore on the day.

We asked the Melbourne Football Club chaplain, Cameron Butler, to marry us, and spent six sessions with him beforehand at pre-marriage counselling. We told him the aim of our wedding was for people to walk away from the day having had fun and felt a connection with the love we felt for each other.

The theme for our wedding was young and vibrant, so we decided on a few radical touches. Our wedding cake was coloured apple green, with a bride and groom in a convertible on the top – the groom even had red hair. My close friend Eleanor asked her mum to make the bridesmaids' dresses and each of the girls chose their own design with the same material. Having been involved with Reach for so long, we had a lot of contacts who helped us with arrangements. Kirk Docker did the music, and another friend, Simon, did the video for us.

The night before the wedding I wanted to be on my own and savour the moment. But try as I might I just kept calling Troy for reassurance. My whole life I'd found it difficult to form attachments to people and now I just wanted to make sure this would be right.

He sent me this text message just before midnight: 'I love you, Toots. Get some beauty sleep.' I hardly got any. In fact I threw up with nerves a couple of times. I love control, and I just wanted the day to go right. I didn't like the feeling that I had to rely on other people. The running sheet for my wedding was six pages long! It was symptomatic of my life to that point.

Troy and I were married on 18 December 2004 at Arlington on Wattle Park. Chris Lamb, Luke Williams, Daniel Bell and Sam Broadbridge were Troy's groomsmen, while my sister Tracey, Kirsten Emes, Emeli Paulo and Carly Schmidt were my attendants. Jim's daughter Matisse and Jim's sister Sharon's daughter Ashlinn were the flower girls. The morning passed without a hitch, but when I arrived I was nervous and couldn't believe this was really happening. I saw Troy waiting patiently, as he always did, in the garden. I was very emotional throughout the whole ceremony. I was so happy I was marrying Troy. I had planned my vows, but when I looked at him I was overwhelmed and could hardly get them out.

I looked into his eyes and said my big speech about why I loved him and wanted to marry him.

Troy
You are my best friend
I promise I'm going to love you no matter what happens
I will always stand by you like you have stood by me.
I love you so much because of everything you've done for me,
For the person that you are,
For the heart that you have,
For the unconditional love,
For your caring nature,
For your determination.
I love you so much Troy, and I promise I'm going to show you that for the rest of our lives.

Until that moment I felt my life had developed a pattern of people leaving me, or of me leaving them. Family and friends had come in and out of my life, with me often leaving as soon as I could. But now I saw my life heading down a different path through my commitment to Troy. He made me feel secure and settled, and I wouldn't need to run away from things any more.

Our wedding was a really happy occasion, more like a party than a ceremony. It was a big fun celebration and everyone mixed well. Throughout the day Troy was so open, and showed me constantly how much he loved me.

So many people said it was one of the best weddings they had ever been to. We danced to 'Feels like Home' by Chantal Kreviazuk which brought the house down. We'd had dancing lessons, and we started off slowly, but after the first turn everyone was very impressed. I struggled a bit as we had only practised in our living room at home and I'd been wearing tracksuit pants rather than a formal dress!

The wedding was a kind of turning point for me and my parents. They were proud of me and I think my dad was pretty stoked that I asked him to walk me down the aisle. It was my way of telling him I was proud of him too – he'd given up drinking. We'd always had a turbulent relationship so I thought it might be awkward walking down the aisle with him, but it wasn't. I was crying and my dad held me up. It was a resolution in a way. I thanked Mum too – I know I was not an easy daughter to raise. Mum was pretty stressed for most of the day, as most mums are at their daughters' weddings!

The wedding was important to Wayne and Pam too. I know they had not always approved of the way Troy and I lived our lives, particularly living together before marriage, but I think they could see how happy and in love we were. During the dance, I'm sure Wayne even had a tear in his eye. It was as if all our past differences might now be put behind us.

After it was all over, Jim and his wife, Sam, drove us to the Duxton in the city. Sam was at the wheel as Jim had had a couple of drinks – he wound down his window and was singing out of the car. He had prearranged to have Frank Sinatra playing for our trip. He took us up to the reception and told them that they had to look after 'a special couple'.

Neither of us slept much that night as we were buzzing about our amazing day. That was unusual for Troy, who loved to sleep, but we could not stop laughing and smiling about the wedding. The next morning when we went down for breakfast Troy forgot to wear his wedding ring. He rushed up to the room to get it as soon as he realised.

At the airport we caught up with Chris Lamb who was flying overseas to meet up with his girlfriend, Lucy, for an extended holiday. Chris had stayed in Melbourne for an extra month to attend the wedding. We both said goodbye to Chris and went to wait at our respective gates, but Troy and I were pretty self-absorbed and didn't make much of a fuss. When I reminded Troy that he didn't know when he was going to see Chris again, Troy rushed off to find him and say a proper farewell. I think about this a lot and am so glad that Troy's last goodbye to his best mate was a proper one. Who would have thought that would be the last time the two friends spoke?

We chose Thailand for our honeymoon because several of our friends had been to Phi Phi Island and loved it. It sounded like the perfect secluded paradise for a honeymoon, and we were looking forward to relaxing together. As it turned out, Wayne and Pam had also honeymooned in Thailand, although we didn't know that at the time.

We arrived in Thailand late at night from Singapore and checked into our resort in Phuket. The next morning we went for a run along the beach. Even though we were on holiday, Troy exercised every day, doing sprints uphill or water running in the hotel pool. We spent several days in Phuket, taking a canoe trip down the river and riding a buffalo, learning Thai cooking, feeding elephants and watching them dance before finally riding one named Bow Bow.

Troy and I loved the Patong shops. We went crazy, getting right into the adrenalin of bartering with the locals as they reached for their calculators. By the end it always became a game. We bought a Von Dutch hat for 100 baht and decided we were going to buy as many as we could from every stall. That night we also bought ninety-seven DVDs!

On 23 December we were off to Phi Phi Island. We arrived by speedboat and were greeted by staff who took our luggage, put leis around our necks, washed our feet and gave us cocktails. Unfortunately we couldn't drink these as Troy was in training and we'd decided not to drink on our honeymoon, but the resort was amazing, and it was as if we had entered heaven.

We took a longboat around to Tonsai Bay, and I pointed out to Troy the number 'twenty' painted on the boat's side. Twenty was our number – Troy's guernsey, our house number, our dog's birthdate – and had brought us so much happiness. It seemed like a good omen.

We spent the rest of the day checking out the village shops and having dinner, and it was dark by the time we jumped in another longboat to go back to the resort. It was pitch black and our driver could not speak English, and I started to get a bit scared. I held on to Troy tightly and asked him what we would do if the boat stopped or we hit something. He said to me, 'Don't worry, we are here together. Hold on to me, and if anything happens we can swim. Or *you* can.' Troy was not the best swimmer, and it was one sport I was better at than Troy. During rehabilitation for his injuries he had to do a lot of swimming, and I made him race me all the time so I could beat him.

The next day we went snorkelling at Maya Bay where the movie *The Beach* was filmed. As an AFL player Troy had done heaps of weights and had a great body and an amazing chest. I thought my husband was hot, and I loved walking around with

Troy and noticing how people admired his body.

We kept Christmas Day mainly to ourselves and talked a lot about our plans for the future. We walked and held hands, discussing our return home and what we would say in our thank you cards to all our wedding guests. Being with Troy I felt so safe, so secure and so in love. I had come a long way since my difficult teenage years, and now I was the luckiest woman in the world. Troy was my handsome, hilarious, caring and sensitive husband, and he would be by my side for the rest of my life.

But you can never really know what is about to happen to you. That evening was the last night we would spend together, and less than twenty-four hours later, my beautiful, loving husband would be gone forever.

Part Three

AFTER THE WAVE

Chapter 12

Coming Home

Coming home to Australia from my honeymoon, without my husband, is the one of the hardest things I have ever had to do.

Mum and I flew into Melbourne on 4 January to a barrage of media interest and attention in my experience of the tsunami. I was amazed by the number of journalists who had gathered at the airport to cover the story, but I was under no illusions that their interest would have been anywhere near as great had Troy not been an AFL footballer. Whether for good or bad, I found myself at the centre of a media storm.

But the most difficult part was not the media, or even meeting our friends and family again; the hardest part was being alone. I was surrounded by people, yet I have never felt so isolated, lonely and unable to connect. In my first week back in Australia, friends and family flocked to my side and were with me night and day. But I knew the day would come when I would be alone in our house, in our bed, and Troy would not be there. Sometimes I went into the bedroom and closed the door on everyone and just howled. And with the grief came the guilt. I knew how many thousands of other people had been affected by the tsunami and that they were all feeling like me. I knew Troy's parents and family were going through hell. Even in those early days, I think I put a lot of pressure on myself to put on a brave face and try to cope, rather than giving myself over to the grieving process.

I am used to doing things my own way and being independent, but for the first month back in Australia I had to let other people do things for me. My cuts were still healing and my upper leg was bandaged and needed constant dressing. A nurse came to wash me each day as I couldn't stand up in the shower, and someone had to rub cream into the scars on my back at regular intervals. I was walking with crutches and couldn't drive. My phone was going all the time and my friends Kirsten, Emeli and Carly became more like personal assistants – one of them was there with me every minute, a pillar of strength. Jacqui Birt and her son Curtis moved in to help me with the cooking and cleaning and Jacqui became like my second Mum. They were all amazingly supportive and I could not have done it without them.

The boys from the footy club were unbelievable on my return. The night I flew back from Thailand, Luke Williams sat and talked to me until 2 am and then sat out in the kitchen after I went to bed to make sure I was okay when I woke up. Luke is very proactive, and at the time he was not in a relationship so he was able to drop everything to help me when I needed it. Troy's teammate Cameron Bruce organised all the players to contribute to a fund which enabled me to get a 24-hour surveillance alarm system, a freezer and an air conditioner. He also walked my dogs every day for the first two months. He did not do it for praise, he did it because Cam is a 'doer'. I remember one afternoon when he returned from walking the dogs I asked him if he would place Troy's Melbourne Football Club guernsey on the casket at the funeral. He said he would be honoured. Later his girlfriend, Jules, told me that he had called her as soon as he got into the car to tell her.

Two days after I arrived home, Jim Stynes and Chris Fagan, the Melbourne football manager, organised a tribute night at the Reach Dream Factory, to remember Troy and also to help the Melbourne boys deal with their team-mate's death. Troy's body still had not been cleared by the authorities to return to Australia and the club felt it was important for the team, their partners and all those in the inner sanctum to come together with some of our closest friends to unite and talk.

I have so many positive memories from that evening. Alistair Nicholson's partner, Julia Foley, spoke about how envious a lot of the partners had been of Troy's and my relationship, and it meant a lot to me to hear how highly they regarded Troy. I also needed to feel the connection with the club, as my life had been so geared around football that it was almost impossible to imagine life without it. I'll never forget Russell Robertson, one of Melbourne's senior players, saying to me, 'You're as much a part of this family as I am.'

Chris Fagan later described the night and Troy in a beautiful speech at the Melbourne Football Club season opener that summed things up perfectly.

From Chris Fagan's speech

For me [the tribute night] was one of the more memorable experiences of my life. Life changing, in fact ... In that room on that night in a very adverse situation I witnessed genuine courage, humour, unity, honesty, compassion, care and sincerity – all characteristics incidentally that embody Troy and the way he led his life.

That night in the most serious of circumstances we showed just how close we are as a club. I always knew it – but that night confirmed it. I remember Neita [captain, Davd Neitz] saying to me at the time that this is what real clubs are all about. He is right. We have high quality people in our organisation, people with excellent values who genuinely care about the wellbeing of our club.

Troy would have been rapt with the occasion. Not because of all the magnificent things we said about him – but because we were together *as one* trying to help Trisha, the Broadbridge family and each other through a very difficult time. This was the sort of environment that he would have flourished in. It was the sort of environment that he strived to create for his team-mates whether playing for the red and blue or with the mighty Sandringham Zebras.

That word 'selfless' was mentioned time and time again in reference to Troy as we eulogised his life during the month of January.

Selfless people like Troy are easy to admire and respect.

They put other people's needs in front of their own.

They encourage rather than complain.

They give praise and build self-esteem rather than criticise.

They persevere through tough times – they don't give up.

They are team players – not individuals.

They are modest – not attention seeking.

They are people of action rather than people of words.

They look to pick you up when you are down.

They are loyal servants.

They get in and do the work required without question.

They are resilient – they make the best of every situation.

They don't take themselves too seriously.

They do the little things that make a difference.

They are givers not takers.

That is Troy's legacy to our club. He led the way in this department. If all of us can aspire to his high standard in this area then our success as a team is ensured.

My first real test following Troy's death came when I had to go into the footy club to empty Troy's locker. Cam Butler, the Melbourne chaplain who had married us, drove me to the club, and I asked my friend Josh Schmidt to come with us. I'd met Josh through Reach so he hadn't known Troy as well as many other people and I didn't feel I had to keep up a strong front for him. I'm glad he was with me. I had driven into the Junction Oval many times but never thought it would be under circumstances like this.

I met Melbourne coach Neale Daniher and Troy's family priest Father Mark in the foyer. I have a lot of respect for Neale and the coaching staff at Melbourne – they had to put aside their own grieving for Troy to support the boys and they handled Troy's death in a really positive way. I know Troy will leave a lasting impression on everyone who knew him at Melbourne, and they will never forget his name or his nature. We made small talk for a while and then Chris Fagan came and took us into the locker room.

All the lockers are painted in club colors and lined up next to each other. From what Troy had told me, he spent a lot of time in the early days talking with Shane Woewodin who had locker number 22, as no one had locker 21 for a while. Troy always spoke so highly of Shane. Then in 2003 along came number 21, Daniel Bell, and what started as locker buddies turned into a great friendship.

Josh and I moved over to Troy's locker and took out all the stuff he'd left behind. In the bottom was his everyday footy gear, player memos from years ago, some letters from supporters, his X-rays and a photo from his early days at Melbourne.

Next I asked if I could have a look inside the gym. The last time I'd been there was a year before our wedding. I'd asked Jim and Sam if Troy and I could take their daughter Matisse to the social cricket match the boys were running. I looked over to the exact spot in the gym where Troy and Matisse had played together and allowed myself to contemplate for a second too long what might have been.

I saw Troy everywhere that day. On the doors of each locker are the names of any hundred-game players who had worn that number. Troy's name was not on the number 20 locker, but it was on the whiteboard where the weights groups were listed.

More than anything that day, seeing his name on that board broke my heart. I thought back over the last five years and how hard he had worked just to get his name written in removable texta on that board. It was such a simple thing but it meant everything to Troy. Having his name on a weights board meant he was part of the team. It meant his dream was real. I kept staring at his name, thinking that at some stage someone would have the job of actually wiping it off. Troy had fought for five years through three shoulder injuries and a knee injury to earn the right to be up there, and soon, with one movement of a cloth, someone would remove his name, wipe him out, just like the wave did.

Chapter 13

World Cricket

My strategy in those early weeks was to keep myself busy and then knock myself out at night with sleeping pills. There were a million details of everyday life that still needed attending to, and in a way it was good to keep busy, but often it was agony. Every time I went home, I was faced with either moving forward or falling into the past. Questions ran through my head: How do I walk the dogs without Troy? How do I fix a leaking tap? How do I manage the shopping now that I am on my own? What do I do with all Troy's clothes? These were small issues but massive problems because they bobbed up everywhere. Letters arrived addressed to Troy, his credit card bills still came in, and in those moments of weakness when I put on our wedding DVD I found myself unable to remember who the smiling girl on the screen was.

The tsunami remained major news well into the new year, and on Jim's advice I hired a media manager, Paul Connors, to help deal with the increasing number of calls which were coming in for me to do television and magazine stories. I was so out of my depth! Paul had handled Jason McCartney when he was seriously injured in the Bali bombings and had heaps of experience. Paul has been great, and it's been reassuring to know someone is looking out for me in a professional sense. With Jim's help, Paul and I began to plan a media approach which enabled us to keep some sort of control over Troy's and my story.

The first major media event I attended was the tsunami benefit cricket match at the MCG on 10 January 2005 between an ICC World XI and Asian XI composed of some of the best cricketers from around the world.

Jim had arranged for me to go into the rooms beforehand and meet the players. It was a great experience, but a bit awkward at first as I didn't really know who any of them were! When I met Brian Lara I had no idea he was so famous until I spoke to Luke Williams afterwards and he told me he was one of the best batsmen in the world and held a cricket record.

Of all the players I met that day, Adam Gilchrist was the one who made the biggest impression. 'You are very brave,' he said. He then asked how I had been sleeping, which was a really good question because without doubt the nights were the hardest. I explained that I had not had any dreams about the actual tsunami yet. Fortunately they did not start till four months later.

'I know it must be hurting inside, but you look well,' he said. 'It seems like you are really coping.'

There was no agenda behind what he was saying. I felt his warmth. He seemed connected to the events and went on to say how I had inspired him. I felt so insignificant but proud when he said that. He gave me hope. He was just so genuine and he spoke really passionately about how Troy's story had affected him. He made me feel in that moment that I deserved to be alive.

When I spoke briefly to the other Australian players I tried to let them know how grateful I was for their efforts but more importantly how I felt they could help the many thousands of others who were suffering. I had never wanted to be the 'face' of the tsunami in Australia, and I was so glad the cricketers talked to me as a person, not as the victim of a tragedy.

When the time came to walk out onto the ground, I gained an insight into why the guys who play at the MCG hold it in such great awe. You are the centre of attention, with 80,000 people focused on you, and I imagined this was the feeling Troy craved. But I would never get a chance to talk to him about it as he would not be running out on the ground again.

I was moved by how many Australians were there. The game was a sellout and the ground was filled to capacity, with around $15 million raised for World Vision. It made me feel really proud to be an Aussie. I sometimes wonder why it takes an event like this to bring people together.

A lot of dignitaries were out on the ground with me before the game, and I was able to thank Steve Bracks for helping my mum get her passport in twenty-four hours so she could come and get me from Thailand. I spoke to the governor general, Major General Michael Jeffery, and thanked him for a letter he had written after Troy's death.

The prime minister was also out on the ground. I found out later that Jim had had a quiet word to one of his minders, as all of a sudden he made a beeline for me and came over and hugged me.

The media cameras went nuts. It was as if we were in a permanent bright light for ten seconds as the flashes went off. I began to realise that all people, no matter who they are or what they do, are basically the same. John Howard is a man with a family, no different to millions of other Australians, and he spoke to me not as the prime minister but as a person who had been touched by the events of 26 December in the same way as everyone else.

In many ways, that was the lesson I took away from that day. Tragedies unite people because at heart we are all the same. The titles people have and the myths we have about each other, created by folklore and the media, are all a bit of an illusion. The reality is that individual life is fragile. Anything could happen to any one of us at any moment, and once you have learned that lesson, each day becomes a real gift. I think maybe that's what drew people together over the tsunami: the fact that it could have happened to anyone. Nature, bad luck, traffic accidents – they don't *choose* their victims. I reckon in life we often forget this, and when a disaster like the tsunami comes along, everyone is reminded again.

Later that night I received a phone call from the Australian Federal Police to say that Troy's body would arrive back in the country on 18 January. They gave me the flight details, as if I could go and pick up my husband, as if he was still alive. It felt ridiculous to be writing the details down. I didn't go. I saw it on the news though, watching my husband's coffin draped in an Australian flag.

The morning after the cricket match, I sat out on my back steps at home, staring at a picture of myself on the cover of the newspaper flanked by Shane Warne and Ricky Ponting. I was smiling, but I almost did not recognise myself. The smiling me in the newspaper was another person, hiding the one inside who was fast shrivelling away. From that moment on I realised there were two Trisha Broadbridges: one who faced the media, and one who could not see how she was going to face the next day.

Chapter 14

The Funeral

Once I had confirmation of the date of Troy's return, we could start to plan the funeral. Le Pine Funerals did most of the organising – they are a sponsor of Sandringham Football Club – and Melbourne Football Club organised the wake. Instead of flowers I asked people to donate to CARE Australia's Tsunami Appeal. Troy's family chose the prayers and the readings and I chose the music. It felt strange to be doing this so soon after I'd organised our wedding, and there was such a strong connection between the two events that I decided to have my skirt made to match my wedding dress top so I could wear it in honour of my husband. Mum organised that for me.

All of Troy's mates from Melbourne would be there, but I knew that Sandringham Football Club had to play a major part also, as the club had been such a big part of our lives. I called the Sandringham captain, Chad Liddell, and left a message asking him to put a Sandy guernsey on Troy's casket alongside Troy's Melbourne guernsey. He called back and seemed surprised and honoured to be a part of Troy's funeral. I'm glad that I made that decision, because I could show the Sandy players and officials how much Troy and I valued the club. I still attend most Sandy games now as I love the family atmosphere, and I feel honoured that everyone makes me feel such a part of the club and supports what I am trying to achieve.

The day before the funeral Emeli took me to the funeral home and I spent some time alone with Troy. I walked up to the casket told him how much I loved him and that I just wanted him to come home. I broke down. I sat on the floor with my head close to his head, grabbing onto the casket because I wanted so badly to reach out to him. I wanted to touch him, to hear him say that he loved me. I told him that I was going to make him proud, and that I would think of him every day. I kept repeating, 'I love you, I love you so much.'

Afterwards Emeli and I talked about our memories. Emeli had lost her mother a few years before and knew something of the pain I was experiencing. I was glad she was there with me.

Chris Lamb flew in from England. It was hard to see Chris again – seeing him come through the doors at the airport was like the final acceptance that Troy was dead. Last time I had seen Chris was with Troy at the airport, and we were all so happy then. So much had changed so quickly.

The inevitable date of 20 January arrived – the day of Troy's funeral. Just thirty-three days after our wedding, I would be burying my husband. I felt absolutely empty that morning. It was as if all the life had been sucked from me and there was nothing left but a shell. Once I was dressed in my wedding dress bodice and a dark skirt, I looked in the mirror and saw the ugly scars on my arms. It was impossible to believe that the face that looked back at me from above the dress that morning was the same one which had looked back from the mirror just a month before.

I sat at my dining-room table with Troy's photo and stared at it in disbelief. Luke Williams said, 'You look beautiful.' They were exactly the same words he had said on my wedding day.

I travelled to the church, St John's Gardenvale, with my family and the bridal party from our wedding. The whole way I was trying to calm myself, but I couldn't get the images of the wedding out of my mind.

Walking into the church was almost impossible. It was silent when we walked in and all I could hear was the sound of my own sobbing. Daniel Bell was alongside me, and for a while it was just us alone in the room with Troy's casket. I couldn't believe I was so close to Troy again. All I wanted was to turn back time and see him rise out of the casket, or if that wasn't possible to lift the lid and get inside with Troy and lie with him.

The church soon filled up, and before long it was packed. The service was beautiful, just like our wedding. Everyone who spoke represented Troy really well. I chose to repeat our wedding vows and let Troy know that, no matter what, I loved him.

> *Troy, you are my best friend. I promise I'm going to love you no matter what happens. I will always stand by you like you have stood by me. I love you so much Troy, and I promise I'm going to show you that for the rest of our lives.*

Jim captured the essence of Troy in a beautiful eulogy.

> *He was the most selfless footballer to play at Melbourne that I can remember.*
>
> *Troy was a genuine guy with an extremely gentle, caring nature, always happy with such a calm presence. A talented footballer brought down in the prime of his career. An amazing son to loving parents Wayne and Pam. An inspirational brother to Sarah, Sam and Jayne. A great friend to many, and in love with such a beautiful woman.*
>
> *Some will remember the way he died, but I'll remember the way he lived, the way he played, and most of all the way he loved.*

On Troy's casket we laid symbols of his life: a wedding photo of us together, a photo of Troy with our dogs, Harry and Sally, a medal he had won in Adelaide for his athletics, and of course his number 20 Melbourne footy jumper, which I had asked Cam Bruce to place on the casket. Chad Liddell came up and put Troy's Sandringham guernsey next to it.

Troy's uncle, John Evans, who had been to Thailand to find the body with Wayne, also read a eulogy which was heard by about a thousand people who had gathered that day at the church and outside. Although I was too overwhelmed to notice on the day, it was amazing to learn later how many people from other football clubs had come to the funeral.

When it came time for the boys to carry the casket out, I knew that many people were experiencing similar pain to mine. It really got to me. I made a commitment then that I would always look out for those men; Troy loved them so much. They are a testament to why Troy was such a good person. What a terrible thing it was for them to have to carry their best friend out of a church.

Hundreds of people gathered outside and formed a guard of honour as the coffin left the church: first the Melbourne boys, standing in a row, and then family, friends and public. My husband was a quiet and beautiful man, and he had a way of bringing people together like that.

The AFL and my manager Paul Connors had put out a brief to the media about the funeral, and to their credit the vast majority respected our request to keep it private, and I will always be thankful for that.

At the burial, when the casket was lowered, I realised I was not ready, I was nowhere near ready to lose Troy. I wanted to jump in there with him. I stood looking down into the grave and I did not want to walk away. I thought, 'Never will I turn my back on him.'

At the wake at the Bentleigh Club there were so many people supporting me. I felt loved, and for the first time since Troy died I began to feel a little less alone. It was beautiful, but even then I wondered how long that feeling could last. I did not want anyone to go home. Jason and Nerissa McCartney were there and we had a connection straightaway – they had an understanding of what I had been through and wanted to help. What amazing people they were to come to Troy's funeral and the wake to support me when they hadn't even met me. I planned to get to know them a lot better.

A memorial service was held the next day in Adelaide for all those who had known Troy in South Australia. I travelled across with Luke Williams, Daniel Bell, Chris Fagan and David Neitz, and as we were checking in at the airport, my phone beeped. It was another Melbourne player, Travis Johnstone, texting 'Thinking of you today'. I was so overwhelmed. Travis and I had been friends for a long time, as he had also attended Reach training, and I have always felt a special bond with him. Not everyone sees the side of Travis that I see – he is a very genuine and caring guy who always gives to others, and when Travis is happy he is flying. For Travis to write this message meant so much to me, and gave me the strength to get on a plane and fly to Adelaide for my husband's memorial service.

Just as we were about to take off, Luke handed me a magazine which he had bought at the airport. It had Powderfinger on the cover, Troy's and my favourite band. Through this small gesture I knew without saying anything that Luke would support me and wanted to lessen the pain for me that day. It's the small gestures from Luke that no one else notices that have really helped me through each day. I know he will never forget Troy.

The service in Adelaide had a real sense of strength about the religious ceremony and I realised how much comfort the Catholic church can offer people in times like this. It was the first time I began to understand why Wayne and Pam are so dedicated to their religion as I really saw how much it means to them and how their lives revolve around the church.

The Melbourne boys sat up the front. I sat with Wayne and Pam, Troy's sisters Jayne and Sarah, and his brother Sam. It was comforting to be part of a grieving family instead of feeling so alone, as if the six of us were in this together. Sarah in particular was great source of strength that day, and for probably the first time since I had met Troy's family, I allowed myself to feel a real connection with them. I felt the Broadbridges had also accepted me, and I realised that they would now be a big part of my life.

Melbourne captain David Neitz read the second half of the eulogy. He was really nervous, even though he performs in front of people each week on the field. In part of his speech, he referred to me as a beautiful person. I was touched. Since Troy's death all I had felt like was an ugly, angry, guilty woman. I had never felt 'beautiful' in my life, I thought only Troy had seen that in me.

I spoke to David after the service and he was inspiring. As both he and Jim kept telling me, while this was a great tragedy it was also a chance to do something really positive with my life in a way that would not only honour Troy, but also put back something into my own life and hopefully the lives of so many others affected by the tsunami.

I returned home to Melbourne that night to find an amazing letter from St Kilda player Max Hudghton. It said a lot of things but above all it said how Max felt that Troy's death had become a symbol for uniting people.

In that moment I made the decision to go back to Thailand and see what I could do to help. I wanted to see Phi Phi Island again. I wanted to walk back over our steps and try to put the voices in my head to sleep.

Chapter 15

Returning to Phi Phi

People could not understand why I wanted to go back to Thailand so soon, and I found it hard to explain. There were just so many unanswered questions in my mind. I suppose what I really needed was to see the exact spot where the wave hit. I needed to make it real in my mind. I needed to see the damage and begin to understand how this tragedy had affected so many other lives like mine.

Since the tsunami I had developed a weird fear of unlikely fatal accidents occurring. Driving a car was hard, so was crossing a road, but taking off on a plane felt like almost certain death to me. So in a way I suppose I was also returning to try and put the enormity of the tsunami into some sort of perspective. I had heard myself telling the story of the wave hitting so many times that I almost did not believe it myself. It all sounded so impossible. Even when I watched footage of the waves hitting other places, it seemed ridiculous that anyone could have recorded it and survived.

By early February the worst of my injuries had healed, so I booked a ticket for 14 February and asked my friend Josh Schmidt to meet me on Phi Phi Island to help document my trip. I wanted him to film the place where the wave hit so I could show others and try to make sense of it myself.

Daniel Bell drove me to the airport. I should have seen the signs even then that I still had a lot of unresolved guilt and grief that I was holding back. Belly was doing his best to keep things light-hearted and make small talk, but I would bounce back with comments like, 'If I die over there, Belly, I want you to make sure I have the same funeral as Troy.' My brain was full of thoughts and irrational fears, and I just said whatever came into my mind at the time without thinking of the effect on Belly. I had such high expectations of him, and I hated the way Troy's death had affected our friendship. Many of my great memories of Troy have Belly in them somewhere, and somehow spending time with Belly just made it even more obvious to both of us that Troy was no longer there. So Belly and I developed this way of avoiding ever really talking about things. Instead we made jokes and tried to hide the pain that way.

At the airport, a whole group of friends was there to see me off. Everyone was in tears as I walked through the doors to customs. I knew people didn't want me to go. I looked back at Belly, Kirsten, Luke, Mel, Leah, Jacqui and Eleanor, said goodbye, and walked off alone.

As soon as I got on the plane I took a sleeping pill and zoned out. Thankfully I slept all the way to Bangkok, because when I arrived I was full of anxiety. I hit a real low point and was ready to get on the next flight back home. Instead I went to sit in the transit lounge and, as you do, I just started looking at people. I watched them as they walked past, some with families, others in couples. I kept looking at their faces, wondering what was going on in their lives. Wondering if they had ever faced real pain.

I realised this was the first time in a long time I had been completely on my own. I started texting people to help me through. Text messages have been a saviour for me: being able to communicate with someone wherever you are, at any time, without actually having to interrupt them. Sometimes I worry that people don't want to hear confronting stories first hand as they have to deal with *the person* as well as the story, so they'd rather read about it first, or hear it from someone else. A text message gives them time to deal with it.

I now try to send a text or an email when I am thinking about someone, or if I hear that someone is having a bad day, or even to thank people for being a friend. A sentence in a text message can make a person's day. I know for me it can put a smile on my face for a least a minute.

I was met at Phuket airport by Johnson O'Shana from the Australian Embassy who had agreed to accompany me back to Phi Phi Island. At my request, the Embassy had found out that Troy's body was discovered in a large water treatment well, in between where we were hit by the wave and where I ended up. As bodies on Phi Phi Island began to be unearthed beneath the debris, they had been tagged with their approximate location before being removed to the morgues.

It was a strange feeling waiting for the speedboat to arrive from Phi Phi Island to pick us up. When Troy and I had last been here the port was packed with people and boats left every twenty minutes. This time around the port was deserted. The room where we had queued for the boat a month ago now echoed with emptiness as I plonked my bags down.

When the speedboat finally arrived, Johnson helped me onboard, but as we sped off, I was suddenly stricken with fear. It had not occurred to me before, but this was the first time I had been back on open water since the tsunami. Not only that, I was travelling across the exact stretch of water the wave would have travelled. The trip from Phuket to Phi Phi takes about an hour and I was petrified the whole way. I hung on as tightly as I could and kept my eyes shut, telling myself that the worst thing that could possibly happen to me in the water had already happened, so this trip would be okay.

When we finally arrived I was drained. I looked down at my phone to find a text message from Nerissa McCartney, saying simply that she was thinking about me and that she admired how strong I was being. I was so glad to hear from her, but I had never felt less strong in my life!

When we got off the boat, I was pleased to see a familiar face. Josh had arrived a day early to help set up and film my return.

That afternoon we had arranged to visit a local school which had not been touched by the tsunami wave but which had lost students in the disaster. I don't know why my instinct had been to visit a school. In our pre-wedding goals, Troy and I had both talked about wanting to help young people, and I guess having worked at Reach for so long, I understood what an impact events can have on a young person's life. I wanted to share what I had learned.

The school was situated on the protected side of the island and the boat ride took about ten minutes. Just ten minutes in the opposite direction an entire village had been washed away, but here on the east side the island was much steeper and so the buildings had been protected when the wave hit.

As soon as we got off the boat and walked up to the school I felt a calmness come over me. As we neared the gates, two little Thai boys were coming down the path in the opposite direction. I waved to them and, as Thai kids do, they smiled and in the most polite manner you can imagine clasped both hands in front of their faces and bowed. I felt an instant connection. Within minutes the kids had dropped their inhibitions and were laughing and playing up for the camera.

That's when it first hit me. I was laughing. For the first time in a month, for a brief second, Troy's death was out of my mind.

It was as if I had been reborn. These kids did not know who Troy was, nor did they expect me to act a certain way. It was absolutely liberating. There was no judgement, no inner toughness, and no gnawing thoughts about how I should act. It was like being five years old again and I loved it.

We entered the school itself and I met with the local teachers, who explained how many of the kids on the island had nowhere to go because the school at Tonsai had been washed away. The school was basically just one building with a dirt patch for a playground and some rusty old swings for equipment. And yet these kids seemed so happy. The more I looked around, the more a plan started to form in my head. I walked into their classroom and started to teach them a little English. I started by writing my name on the board: Trisha Broadbridge. I felt proud to write it, as though Troy and I were starting off on something together. Each of the kids wrote down their names and then one little boy came up and gave me a folded piece of paper. I unfolded it and it was a Valentine's Day love heart.

It was a lesson I will never forget. Here were these kids, in a third-world school, having lost classmates, friends, and family, and yet they were still smiling and willing to give love. And here was I, living in my big house with my nice car and all the support systems you could imagine, absolutely unable to cope.

In that moment I decided the only way I was going to get better was to start giving. I didn't exactly know what, but I knew it was what I had to do.

The more I looked around, the more a plan started to form in my head. I asked the teachers what I could do to help improve things, and they said they needed more books and new play equipment. But that was just the start. My mind was racing. In my mind, I drew a mental picture of what this school needed. And I sort of took it upon myself to make this my little project for Troy, to help the people of Phi Phi Island.

That afternoon, Josh filmed while I played soccer with the kids. They were just the same as kids anywhere. They laughed and showed off and I did the same. As the sun set that afternoon, I started to dream. It was important for me to give hope somewhere, even if it was just for myself. Somehow, out of the depths, some good needed to rise, and for us this was it. That afternoon, the Reach Broadbridge Fund was born.

Before I returned home, I had one last hurdle to cover in Thailand. I needed to see the spot where Troy's body was found.

We were staying in the same resort on Phi Phi that Troy and I had stayed at, which had not been damaged in the tsunami. For some reason I had asked the hotel manager to put me in the same room that Troy and I had been in. I know that Josh was worried about me, but I wanted to feel as close to Troy as I could. I knew logically that it was too soon for me to be back on Phi Phi, but I couldn't explain to people the pain that was in my head. I had to see the spot where Troy had died. I had to relive the experience in order to make sense of it.

On the morning of 15 February 2005, I set out on the long walk back to Tonsai Bay. Although Josh was with me to film the walk, it felt like a lonely forty-five-minute trek to Tonsai where the wave had hit. Each time I walked past a side track signposted to Lana Bay or some other destination, I had the strongest physical sensation that I wanted Troy to be with me and we would take one of those turns instead of the one we took to Tonsai Bay. I can't tell you the grief of knowing how a simple little left-hand turn could change your life so dramatically.

When we emerged from the jungle onto the beach, the waters were impossibly calm, but it was also clear that the clean-up would not be finished for years. The walk along the rocks up to the actual beach was made more difficult by the amount of strange debris still scattered around the water's edge. All the way along I saw camera film, credit cards, sunglasses, DVDs, shirts, pots and pans, fishing traps, boat parts. There was no real pattern to it, it seemed to reflect the random way the wave had struck and blown away everything in its path.

When we made it to the main beach it was totally deserted. In the village itself there might have been a dozen people left. The few concrete buildings left standing were just shells, and as far as the eye could see there were piles of rubble and debris.

I stood for a moment to get my bearings and work out exactly where Troy and I had walked that day. It was hard to figure out because none of the landmarks I might have used had survived the wave. I found the frame of a 7-Eleven still standing, though the contents were gone. I remembered running to that 7-Eleven during dinner the night we had first gone to Tonsai because I cut my finger opening a bottle of water and needed to get bandaids. The drama of cutting my finger seemed ridiculously trivial now.

Eventually I calculated the exact spot where the wave had hit us. I walked to that spot. I was numb. In some ways I could feel Troy with me, and yet the more I tried to imagine it the further away he felt. I stood for about thirty minutes in that spot and then made my way a further 400 metres up the beach to where Troy's body had been found.

As I was walking I kept thinking how far it seemed on foot, and yet how little time it had taken in the wave. Between where Troy and I had been standing and where he ended up there were about three destroyed buildings and dozens of uprooted coconut trees.

As I neared the treatment well, I felt the urge to climb down to the bottom. All the water had been drained and so without thinking I walked down. I couldn't believe my beautiful boy had ended up with so many others, down here among all the debris.

Phi Phi after the tsunami – the wave hit us on the beach to the right.

After the wave the island looked deceptively calm.

The debris will take forever to clear from the island.

This is where I was waiting to be evacuated from Phi Phi by helicopter. Everyone tried to shield their wounds from the sand.

People who were not injured waited to be evacuated by ferry. I searched the queue for Troy.

I took this when I went back to Phi Phi.

With Pang Pond – whenever I return to Phi Phi, the kids help me to get life in perspective.

Chapter 16

Falling

When something as shattering as the tsunami happens to you, it is as if all the experiences of your life come together to either make or break you. I would love to be able to say that after revisiting Thailand I was able to put things to rest and move on with my life, but it didn't work out like that.

Little things popped up every day, reminding me of Troy and of how much I missed our love. Every time I got into Troy's car, I went to adjust the seat, which I no longer needed to do. Almost everything in the house had some meaning in terms of my life with Troy. Some objects, like the little white teddy bear which now sits on Troy's grave, were full of memories of the old me. I'd bought the bear for Troy when he went on his first interstate trip, a practice game for Melbourne at Subiaco, so he would know that I was thinking about him. He told me that on interstate trips the bear used to remain hidden and squashed in his football bag, to keep it out of sight of the other players. Now the bear is now not only a bit out of shape, it also has a permanent smell of sweaty socks.

The memories of Troy were already fading in stupid ways. At times I physically felt his arm around me, drawing me in, and then I would look down and see nothing. It's hard to explain to people, but that 'nothing' is the thing that lasts, not the sensation of Troy being there. I tried to tell myself and others that the memory of Troy was strong and would get me through, and yet when I saw couples in love, the memory didn't even come close.

I would weep when I got out of my self-indulgent state and remember there were 300,000 other families affected this way. I found it hard to accept there was so much pain in the world.

I was seeing a psychologist for grief counselling, and as the weeks wore on it was as if people started expecting me to be normal again. So I would put on my 'other me' face. I'd go out and talk to people in supermarkets and at the footy club. I would try to be positive and a role model for the younger kids who followed my story, but deep down I was just a girl who had lost the love of her life and could not see how she was going to get through the next ten minutes, let alone the next ten years.

The pain was so constant and consuming, I felt like I was running across quicksand and the moment I stopped to think, I would sink.

And sink I did.

In mid March, Belly and I went to visit Jim who was having a small get-together to celebrate the birth of his son Tiernan. Because Troy and I had planned to start a family that year, the pain was unbelievable and took me by surprise. I had not expected this at all.

That night I went out drinking, and the next day I felt I needed to go to Troy's grave and tell him how I felt. So Kirsten drove me out to the cemetery and we lay there together. It was a beautiful sunny day, but I felt a long way from beautiful. I lay on the grass at Troy's headstone and talked, and in my heart I was telling him that I would be there to see him very soon.

I am so alone, but surrounded by people. I feel so unloved, I miss Troy so much, I am nothing without him, I have no purpose and have no feeling in my heart.

I don't want to go to bed at night, I don't want to lie in bed by myself, I have not gone to bed alone in so many years. No one will lie in bed with me, hold me.

Why has this happened to us? We were so happy, so in love.

Now I will never have a family, never have anyone that loves me, that touches me, that will take care for me.

I am so scared, I wish I never survived, I wish I was dead as I am in so much pain, and eventually everyone will get on with their lives and I never will be able to get on with mine.

I will never be able to live a normal life, no one will ever understand my pain, the hurt the longing for Troy. To touch him, to smell him, to talk to him, to share the experience of the wave.

It is so hard to explain that feeling. Despite all the people who helped me during that time, I have never felt so alone. In the days after the tsunami, I read in the papers about how brave I was, but that wasn't me at all. I was a total mess. Sometimes I think people wanted to believe I was brave just so *they* could cope. It makes it easier for the world if the survivors of tragedy are courageous. But I guess I thought I should be braver than I was – it was like I expected myself to be a superwoman. I was someone who had always been cool in a crisis, as long as I had somewhere to focus my attention. The tsunami itself, my survival on the steps up to the Viewpoint, the hospital, the return home – all those experiences had given me a focus, a crisis to get over. But nothing prepared me for what happened next.

As a teenager, I'd suffered from the 'alcohol blues'. I'd go out drinking with girlfriends and we'd be really depressed the next day and would forget that it was the alcohol talking. I didn't realise then that alcohol is a depressant – we thought our depression was real.

This time was different. I got drunk again, but the next day it wasn't the alcohol talking. My pain was real.

I woke up alone in bed. Troy was not there to hold me, and he never would be ever again. This was how I would feel every morning. Once the dust had settled, it would just be me, alone in my house, with pictures of Troy hanging on the walls.

I sat on the bed with a whole bunch of pills in front of me and the phone in my hand. I rang my mum, hysterical, and told her to get over here because I was going to hurt myself.

Kirsten was outside and I screamed out to her from the bedroom. She came in and asked what was going on. I kept yelling, 'I can't do it! I can't do it!' I was emotionally and physically in pain.

I ran into the kitchen wailing. I was desperate not to feel this way. I was angry. I screamed at Kirsten, 'You don't understand! You don't understand!' Jacqui was home too, and Kirsten and Jacqui were trying to calm me down, but I felt boxed in and backed into a corner, and I lashed out and hit the window. I looked around and grabbed at the knife block.

I rang my mum and the first thing I said is, 'You need to come here. I want to die, and Jacqui and Kirsten won't let me.'

I talked at Mum, not to her. It was ridiculous. We discussed how I was going to kill myself. It was almost like my mum was helping me, but she was just trying to keep me calm and play along. I honestly believed that my mum was going to arrive with a gun. Kirsten rang her stepfather and explained what was happening and he told her to ring the police or a clinical assessment team immediately.

They told Kirsten to drive me straight to the hospital. Mum and Dad drove over to Cheltenham, and by then I had calmed down enough to know I needed help. Kirsten and Jacqui drove me to the hospital, and I must have looked a real mess as I walked up to the reception desk. I was wearing a Melbourne fleecy jumper, my face was covered in tears, and if ever someone looked like they needed help it was me.

What happened next frightens me to write. I am sure my memory of the events is somehow wrong, because I just can't accept that people in trauma can only get this level of support. After waiting over an hour a psychiatrist finally came to see us. Kirsten and Jacqui came in with me to the interview room, and the guy's opening question was, 'So tell me why you want to kill yourself. Don't you know you have so much to live for?' Things got worse from there. In fact the interview was so bad, Kirsten and I started to laugh. Maybe that's the technique they use these days, but during the interview, I felt the only way I could show this guy how serious I was would be to kill myself right then and there.

I'm not proud of what I did next, and I mean no disrespect to the psychiatrist who treated me, but I just had to stand up and leave. I wanted to run to the beach and drown myself and be with Troy forever. I pushed my way past and headed for the door. In my mind I was going to take the very first chance I had to kill myself.

At that point a security guard walked in and had to restrain me and they took me to a room. A nurse entered the room and sedated me. They certified me there and then, which meant that under the *Mental Health Act* I was not a voluntary patient and was not allowed to leave.

My mobile phone rang. It was my psychologist who I had been seeing for grief counselling. After a long conversation she asked me a straight question: 'Is this the role you want to play for young people?' I flipped out when she said that. It was true, I was being so weak and such a failure. I just lost it and started screaming.

Five hours later, I woke up and was told that I would be going to Albert Road Clinic. Thankfully they had booked me under a different name, as the media could have had a field day if they'd got hold of the story. I was under twenty-four-hour care, on full suicide alert.

The first person I spoke to on the ward was a male nurse. He opened by telling me that I had been committed and could not leave the room without his permission. Anything I could potentially harm myself with was taken away. Looking back I understand why he had to do this but I felt so degraded. I was not supposed to end up in a place like this.

They did a full physical examination. I had to strip down to my underpants and while I was on the bed they proceeded to look for weapons. It didn't feel safe. I just kept thinking, 'I don't belong here. How did I get to this point?'

The next day Luke Williams came in to see me. The look on Luke's face was extraordinary, like we were in this together. Luke didn't stay long, but as he left it became all too real to me: I walked him to the door, but I couldn't leave. I felt ashamed and embarrassed.

I just sat inside those four walls, certified crazy. Maybe home wasn't that bad after all, I thought, even without Troy. Kirsten was with me most of the time, but I felt really low and anxious. How was I going to get back up? I was defeated, I couldn't hurt myself even if I wanted to. At one stage they let me go out onto the balcony and I realised that it was enclosed by perspex. 'It stops the jumpers,' said a nurse.

That night I talked to the nurses and began to get an insight into how places like Albert Road worked. They mentioned that a lot of people liked coming in because they were getting cared for, and that is part of the reason they treat you so harshly when you arrive. After that I had a respect for the nurses. They had to be tough with me, but it had really scared me.

After talking to a hospital psychiatrist, I agreed to check into a ward and was taken off the certified list. I could have walked out at any time but I stayed for five days and had some rest. I realised that I probably hadn't slept for a week.

The media still didn't know I was in there. The following week I was to be part of the pre-match events for a tribute match to Troy, and I had agreed to do some media appearances, but Paul told them I was unavailable for a few days and they respected that. I had to be careful that I didn't wander around the wards in case someone recognised me, and I had to remember I was in under an alias.

The psychiatrist interviewed Mum and Dad and Kirsten. He laid it on me that I had done this for attention. I wasn't having a good run with psychiatrists and psychologists. After interviewing them he came in and started delving into my past. I was just so pissed off, I blurted out all this stuff I had been thinking.

'Don't you understand what has happened?' I said. 'I was in love and married this guy and he was killed in a once-in-a-thousand-year freak. What has that got to do with my past? This is now. I am not coping. What do people expect me to do? Every day I have the same frustration. It's all I think about, and right now I can't see myself thinking about anything else. Ever.'

Part of my therapy was to sit down and write a list of things I needed to change when I got home. The first thing I wrote was that I had to stop drinking to escape the pain. I also wrote that I needed to do more exercise and try to involve myself in as many all-consuming tasks as possible. But I knew my mind wouldn't be fooled by that. For me, surviving the wave was the easy part. What else could I have done but survive? It was just luck. Climbing the stairs was easy, I was driven by the love of Troy, driven by the hope of finding him. What was hard was finding a reason to live knowing that Troy wasn't there any more.

So it came down to this moment. Sitting in isolation under suicide watch, unable to see a single reason to go on.

Jim's visit to Trisha in Albert Road Clinic

I found out Trisha had tried to harm herself when Kirsten rang me the morning after. In some ways I wasn't surprised. Trisha had a history of depression, and in our discussions since Troy died she had mentioned how some nights she went through hell.

After the tsunami, I noticed Trisha had adopted an old life skill of hers which involved turning off her emotions. I've seen it a lot in young people who have experienced pain. Rather than face the pain head on, they shut down. It's a natural reaction.

All her life Trisha had refused to rely on other people. She is an incredibly strong person like that, but it is also a weakness of hers that she cannot ask for help. So when she finally allowed herself to be vulnerable with Troy, it was the first time she had ever let anyone into her life in a way which made her open to really being hurt. Even at school Trisha had never entirely fitted in. She was a very complex girl and would have tested any parent. I think all those who knew and loved her were happy when she finally found balance with Troy.

After giving Trisha a couple of days to have some time to herself, we went to the clinic to see her. I took my wife Sam and daughter Matisse as I thought seeing them would be a help.

I have been to Albert Road Clinic a few times so I knew what to expect. What I didn't expect was to see Trisha sitting on her bed, smiling at us as we walked in.

'I stuffed up, Jim,' she said.

'It's okay,' I replied. And I think that was enough for her to hear.

Trisha's parents were in there with her and as usual Trisha was being really open about how she felt and what had happened. You always know where you stand with Trisha. It was weird, but classic Trisha. It was like visiting her in a hotel room on holiday. She talked through the events of a few nights ago and got it all off her chest. She told us how the Albert Road psych had advised her to get off the depression medication she had been placed on. This made sense: it had been as if Trisha was being treated for depression when the real problem was that she should have been grieving.

I then recognised something I had seen a lot in football. When your story becomes public property, it is really hard to grieve, or recover, and sort through your issues. It is as if the media is doing it for you sometimes. All the time Trisha was in the limelight she was acting, as she had done most of her life. She was playing the strong widow, when deep inside she was just a little 24-year-old girl who had found the love of her life, and then lost him in a moment.

I think the time in Albert Road Clinic was great for Trisha. It gave her respite from the pressure of having to cope. It allowed her to grieve in her own way rather than how she thought people wanted her to be. Because of his AFL profile, Troy became public property and so had Trisha. It was as if Troy was the conduit for many members of the public to feel a connection to the tsunami and I think Trisha felt she was carrying that weight of expectation.

After Trisha's parents left, Matisse played on the floor at Trisha's feet, while Sam and I sat on the bed and just talked.

'No one is judging you for what has happened.' I said. 'It's okay. What happened last night is okay.'

I didn't need to say much else. I have known Trisha a long time and despite all the hiccups along the way, the one thing she has always been able to do is get back on track and keep on moving forward. It was almost like this moment was the time she was able to say to herself: 'This thing has happened to me and I no longer need to fight it. It is part of who I am and by letting myself feel the pain, I am also allowing myself to heal.'

While I sat resting and recovering in that ward, I really had to make some decisions. I wanted to start work on the Reach Broadbridge Fund, and sort out exactly what that would be. I had to face the media again soon. My first commitment was an interview with the *Footy Record* about the tribute match the day after I was due to go home, and I knew I had to be really positive for the boys' sake. I was not feeling at all strong in myself, but I'd lived with a footballer and I knew the importance of maintaining focus leading up to a game. There was no way I was going to lose it: it was about them, not me.

Chapter 17

Paying Tribute

On Easter Sunday, 26 March 2005, Melbourne played Essendon at the MCG in Round 1, and the club dedicated the game to Troy. The significance of those two teams playing each other in the first round was massive – Troy's first AFL game had been against the Bombers, and his last game for Melbourne was also against Essendon, in the finals. I was to give a short speech at the pre-match dinner, and Jo Juler, the media and communications manager at Melbourne, had also kindly asked me to toss the coin for the start of the game. For the second time that year, I would be walking out onto the MCG in front of a packed house.

I'd only been out of Albert Road Clinic for a week, and was feeling so nervous I couldn't sleep at all the night before. I just kept running through all the things I had to do on the night and hoping I didn't stuff everything up. I'd even spent most of the previous evening practising the coin toss. It was stupid, but I couldn't bear it if I lost the toss!

Although the coverage I've received since the tsunami has

really helped me, and most of it has been positive, on that day more than any I wished the focus was all on the players. Even as I snuck out the back door to go to the hairdressers, I prayed that my being at the ground would not distract the players in any way. Troy would have hated that, he was never one to take the limelight. Today was a day for the players, not one for the 'tragic bride'.

At the hairdresser's that morning, I asked them to run red streaks through my hair. Redheads, the match company, were the game-day sponsor, and I thought I should go red for the occasion too.

My parents and brother drove me to the game and on the way we picked up Jim. When we arrived at the ground the gates were still locked and we had to talk our way inside. As we stood in the stands waiting, just about everyone who passed us had a second glance or even stared openly, which was a strange feeling. I had never experienced anything like that before.

We were invited to the pre-match dinner as guests of the Melbourne Football Club, and I was seated at a table with Troy's family and the club chaplain, Cam Butler, who had been amazing throughout the whole ordeal, supporting both me and the players and their partners. I had been trying hard to cover my nerves by cracking jokes, but the moment we walked into the function room I was overcome with grief. I didn't know where it came from. There was a tension hanging over the place, as if no one knew quite how to act and what to say. Troy and I had spent many post-match functions together in this room over the last six years. I just never thought I would be walking in there with that atmosphere.

The dinner started with a beautiful video tribute to the community of AFL. It highlighted the fact that football is more than what happens in the four quarters, it's about the supporters, players and players' families. I saw Troy's handsome face on the screen and also Jason McCartney, Ted Whitten and Ron Barassi. Outwardly I was so proud of Troy. He was so quiet in his own way and now he was having such a huge impact, and in some ways it was great to have the footage to look back on. But on the inside, it just burned with pain whenever I saw him on DVD or heard his voice. It still drives a stake through my heart that I can see him and hear him, but I can never touch him again or talk to him just to tell him how my day went.

After the presentation Tim Costello, the chief executive of World Vision, spoke about his experiences of the tsunami. I was glad he spoke because he made the point that there was a community of suffering around the world, not just one person and not just the Australians who were killed, but hundreds of thousands who had suffered. Tim also made a really good point that I had never considered. He said that most Australians were fully aware of how fit and strong AFL athletes were, so the fact that Troy was just swept away was an indication of how strong the tsunami was, and he felt it had helped Australians understand the power of the whole thing.

When it came my turn to speak, I felt emotionally shattered. But I stood and moved towards the microphone, and with each step I seemed to find a new strength. I started by talking about how much the Melbourne Football Club had meant to Troy. He was just a kid when he arrived from Adelaide, and the club had taken him in all those years ago. Through all his injuries and self-doubts, the club had been there for him. Troy had always pointed out that the club was nothing more than the people in it, and it was the people that made the Melbourne Football Club such a special place for us. Troy had talked a lot about the mateship of training and playing together, of sharing the highs and lows, particularly with the other young players, and how he and his friendships had grown stronger as a result.

Standing up there in front of all those people, I really felt a part of something. But in many ways that feeling of belonging is what makes life in the AFL so bittersweet. While the players are on the team, they are a part of something special, but eventually it is someone else's turn and I know many of them find it massively hard to move on. As I spoke that day, I became aware of one of my own fears: I was not ready to move on from the Melbourne Football Club myself. I needed that place like nothing I could imagine, and at that moment it seemed more important than my own family.

I am not a great public speaker but towards the end of my talk, half the room had tears in their eyes. I finished by thanking those who had stood beside us, and told everyone how much I loved being a part of this family. As I walked back to my seat the room erupted in applause.

None of the players were at the dinner as they were preparing for the game, but I remembered the words Cam Bruce had said to me at my lowest point: 'Trisha, I just want you to know, me and the boys are in this for the long haul.' Those words saved my life at the time. And just as I was thinking that, my phone beeped. To my amazement it was a text message from David Neitz. It just said, 'We are going to play tough tonight, see you out on the ground.'

Before the game, Jim and I were taken down onto the boundary line with Troy's brother and sisters, Sam, Sarah and Jayne, to watch the boys run out. Jim and I did a couple of radio interviews, but I was so anxious I can't even remember what I said. The AFL played a tribute to Troy on the big screen, and I could feel the eyes of the crowd directly behind us boring into me. It was a funny sensation: the tribute was so public and yet so private as well. Two of Troy's mates, Luke Williams and Cam Bruce, spoke on the video, and I could see the way they struggled to keep it together. It was almost as if they were looking straight at me in front of all these people and saying, 'Trisha, we really know what you are feeling, because we are feeling it too. We are in this together.'

When the tribute finished, they released 2000 red balloons.

Usually at the start of a game, the two teams run out onto the ground from separate gates, but tonight, as a tribute to Troy, they would both walk out together. I don't really know Kevin Sheedy or much about Essendon, but I will always be thankful for that gesture.

I stood at the edge of the race feeling a bit awkward, not really sure what my role was. Jim was with me, but I didn't know whether I should look at the players or if that would be a distraction. Being a footballer's wife I knew that they are so professional that sometimes you just have to stay in the background. But as the players walked out they made the decision for me. James Hird, the Essendon captain, looked me straight in the eye as he emerged and just gave me a nod. It was almost as if he was saying, 'It's okay, you have a right to be here,' and from then on things just flowed.

The warm-up lasted about three minutes. I was standing on the ground with Jo Juler, waiting to be told what to do next. They were the longest three minutes you could imagine. When the players finished their warm-up they came together in two lines. I was content to watch from the boundary, but unbeknowns to me, the expectation was that I should stand alongside the players. Jo pushed me forward, and little me walked up to David Neitz as they prepared for the on-ground tribute.

David is a beautiful man, but he is also 6 foot 4 inches tall and weighs about 100 kilos. 'It looks like you've got a partner,' I said as he took me across to the line-up. David put his great arm around me and said, 'I'd be honoured.'

In the line you could literally feel the energy of the players. The rooms of an AFL club prior to game time are always full on, but I can only imagine what they were like before this opening round when the game was a tribute to a team-mate who has passed away. All week the media had been saying events could turn against the Demons if they let themselves be overawed by the emotion of the day, but now I knew the opposite had happened, that the boys were ready to focus on the game and win for Troy. Any thought that the boys had tried to block out the events of Troy's death disappeared. I was so proud. This was their tribute to him and they were all in.

As soon as the announcer started to speak and said Troy's name I felt David hold me closer. It was his way of saying, 'We're standing here with you.' I looked to the ground, then up to the Essendon team. I was face to face with the players. I felt like I was ready to go into battle myself.

To end the tribute they played the national anthem, which was my cue to walk to the middle of the ground and toss the coin. In the centre square, James Hird came up to me and offered his sympathies on behalf of the Essendon Football Club. I was just so impressed with the way he conducted himself.

When it came to tossing the coin, however, I was far from a class act. I had been practising all week for this moment and then the impossible happened. The umpire looked at me and asked for the coin. I froze. I had no idea I was supposed to bring a coin! In desperation I turned to Jim, who in typical Irish fashion shrugged his hands and looked over at one of the photographers, who thankfully produced a twenty-cent piece.

With the crowd and the television waiting, umpire Darren Goldspink took control and flipped the coin himself. To my great relief the Demons won. David Neitz pointed to the railway end of the MCG and I just couldn't wait to get off the ground. Jim kept trying to hold me back because I was going so fast. 'Trisha,' he said, 'you are living every young kid's dream here, walking on the MCG. Take your time.'

The match itself was a bit of a blur. I sat up with the players' group, accompanied by Jim, Luke, Belly, my friend Eleanor and a group of the players' wives and girlfriends. When the siren sounded to start the game, I had a really strange feeling. It was almost like that siren signalled the end of Troy's time at Melbourne. The new season had started and I felt that Troy and I were yesterday's news.

Right at that moment I looked at Luke, who was shattered at not being picked for the game. 'I can't do this,' I said to him with tears rolling down my cheeks.

'Yes, we can, Trisha.' That was all he said, but the way he said 'we' made me feel that, even then, I was not alone.

From the first bounce you could see how committed the Demons were that night. Clint Bizzell later described it as playing with no fear for their own safety. While this is nothing new to the AFL, I suspect there are levels of intensity, and that night the Melbourne Football Club was at its most intense.

When the siren sounded to end the game, Jim took me down to the players' race. The boys were so happy as they came off the ground, and I was proud of the way they had played and won. As soon as they saw Jim and me, they all hugged and kissed me before heading into the room. The last player in was Cam Bruce. I think he waited until last because he knew how special this was, and before I knew it he had dragged me down into the rooms.

Once inside, Neale Daniher grabbed me and pulled me into the circle where the players sang their victory song. Being in that circle, singing that song, was the most real I had felt in two months. When something tragic happens, you tend to close down emotionally on many levels. You certainly feel masses of pain, but it is almost as if you forget how to feel happiness. That circle of joy was just a glimpse, but it was such a relief.

On so many levels, the change rooms of an AFL football team are no place for a woman, but the after-match speech room is even more out of bounds, so when Neale Daniher asked me if I wanted to address the team, I was flabbergasted.

When the doors closed behind us, there I was in this room with the boys. Neale went over the game, praising the players and reviewing the weak points as well, and then he looked straight at me and said, 'I think it is appropriate that Trisha has the final words.'

Unlike the pre-match dinner, this time I felt massively strong. To stand up in front of those boys who I so admired, to know they had just played their hearts out for me and for Troy, was a high of unbelievable proportions. I knew they were proud as well. The way they had played and won the game when they were under so much pressure was a credit to them.

To be honest, I can't remember much of what I said, only that I ended by speaking for Troy. I was so proud to be a part of the Melbourne Football Club that night, and Troy and I will be proud to be a part of the club forever.

Part Four

Beyond the Wave

Chapter 18

The Reach Broadbridge Fund

Over the next few months, I surrounded myself with good friends and mentors and immersed myself in the management of the Reach Broadbridge Fund. We decided the aim should be twofold: to take the Reach Foundation to South Australia, Troy's home state, which had been a long-term dream of Troy's; and to create an education centre on Phi Phi Island in Troy's name. Both aims needed money, so I set myself the task of getting it.

Our first task was to work out whether we could build over in Thailand using Thai labour and Thai materials. After lots of discussion we decided against this, because much of Thailand was still recovering from the tsunami and we could not guarantee the job would be done properly or on time. We opted to use a local Australian company, Aarons Outdoors, which specialises in building large and small bungalows. Owner Aaron Giddings contributed their time and provided the materials at cost. Aaron turned out to be a great choice for the Phi Phi project, because he understands what it means to run your own business. He started out building dog kennels and developed his business over ten years to a stage where he now runs a huge factory in Moorabbin and has four outlets around Melbourne.

When I was in Thailand I had put together a wish list of things to be built. With Aaron's help, we designed a three-room fifteen-metre bungalow which was to become the Broadbridge Education Centre. Part of the building was to be a mini library, as I wanted to help the Thai kids learn English, which would be a massive advantage when it came to the tourist trade which I hoped would flourish in Thailand again before too long. Aaron and his business partner Mark also helped us by designing and donating a playground full of play equipment.

The plan was to build the bungalow in Melbourne, place it in a container and then ship it over to Thailand and assemble it there. Fortunately we were able to find a shipping company willing to contribute containers. Even as we discussed the construction of the site, it began to seem real in my head. I knew there was still a heap of work to do, but I also knew that with the right people behind me, we could make this happen.

The more the project became a reality, the more I realised that even with all the contributions we were receiving, this project was going to cost every cent of the $150,000 we had budgeted. We needed to raise more money.

Perhaps the biggest fundraising disappointment was an event we ran the night of Troy's tribute game. We had over twenty people working from the Reach office, ready to answer phones when the number was read on air before the game. The TV coverage was fantastic, but when it came time to flash up the number, it was only on the screen for about ten seconds. We got one phone call that night, a little kid who contributed eight dollars, and for the rest of the night the phones were silent. In the end we lost $100 because we had promised to feed the volunteers!

I learned a valuable lesson. Raising the money and profile to get the education centre built was not going to be easy. If the Reach Broadbridge Fund was going to work, I was going to have to drive it. However I was uncomfortable with using the tsunami as bait for my fundraising. This was really important to me – I would rather not have gone ahead than offended people, particularly survivors or people who lost loved ones in the tsunami. Fortunately Michelle McQuaid and Katherine Ellis from Reach put together a really strong media strategy.

Slowly but surely the fund was moving closer to the mark we needed to build the education centre, but we were still about $30,000 short of making it a reality.

One day out of the blue I met Kate Hildebrand at Reach and showed her some of the footage from my trip back to Phi Phi. Kate and her husband Ross own an earthmoving company based on the Gold Coast, and they are benefactors of Reach and had been particularly generous in supporting Reach's efforts to begin offering programs in Queensland. In my life I have met lots of good people, but these guys are beyond that. They are not multimillionaires, but they have huge hearts.

The day after Kate had seen the DVD she left a message on my mobile saying she had news for me. I rushed into the office and asked my friend Paige Davies, who was also a program manager at Reach, to leave a message for them, then sat by the phone. When it rang, I was so excited I nearly ripped it off the desk.

It was Kate. 'Hi, Trisha, how are you?'

My heart was thumping. I knew Kate and Ross had contributed to Reach before, but I didn't dare allow myself to think they would contribute to the Reach Broadbridge Fund as well. After the events of the past months, I no longer took anything for granted, but for the first time since the tsunami I found myself searching and hoping for good in the world. And boy, did I find it.

'I spoke to Ross last night, and we think we might be able to help the school in Thailand. How much are you short?'

'Thirty thousand,' I blurted, barely able to control myself.

'Well, consider the project on,' said Kate. 'Our family got together and agreed to sponsor the project. There will be a cheque in the mail tonight.'

It's hard to explain what a relief it was to hear those words. The Melbourne Football Club had helped me on a personal level by paying out Troy's contact for 2005–2006, which gave me some financial security and ensured I wouldn't lose the house. But this final contribution from the Hildebrands meant I could now turn around and start doing good for other people. I have thought of Kate and Ross many times since that day, and I hope they know how much their contribution meant to me. The Broadbridge Education Centre was now a reality.

Meanwhile we were also trying to raise the money to bring Reach programs to South Australia. Paige and I were on our second explorative visit to Adelaide and had just about given up on raising the funding we needed when a call came through from Katherine Ellis, General Manager, Reach. The Department of

Education in South Australia were giving us a grant of $38,000 to run two teacher training workshops and one leadership workshop for teenagers. It was really going to happen: in September Reach would have its first presence in South Australia.

We still had a lot of work to do, but the hard part was over. Troy's dream of bringing Reach to his home state was about to come true.

Chapter 19

One Step Back, Two Steps Forward

The dream of returning to Thailand to build something when so much had been destroyed there helped give me a focus, but I was still daunted by the thought of having to rebuild my life and recreate Trisha Broadbridge. I felt like a teenager again, as if I had to make a new life for myself because the old one didn't work without Troy. But deep in my heart I knew that at some stage – in six months, twelve months, two years, whatever the timeframe – I was going to have to accept what had happened and move on.

A number of positive experiences helped me through this time. In early April I was asked to unveil the VFL premiership flag before Sandringham's first home game for 2005. Even though the wind was not on my side and it did not happen as smoothly as I had hoped, I was a proud woman that day standing before Troy's Sandy team-mates. I felt at home. The Round 2 game against Port Melbourne was dedicated to Troy, with all the players wearing black armbands. The players made a pact that they would give everything that day to show Troy how much he was respected, and they were determined to win no matter what. In a replay of the grand final, once again Sandy beat Port. Luke Williams played the best game I have ever seen him play – in my eyes, he was the difference between the two teams on the day. He stood tall for his mate Broady. I hugged Luke tight after the game, because I was so proud of him after the difficult couple of months he had had. He really shone in a time of adversity.

It was announced that the best Melbourne-listed Sandringham player would win the Troy Broadbridge Trophy at the end of the year, at Melbourne's Best and Fairest awards. It is such a fitting trophy to be named after Troy!

Earlier I had received a letter from the Canadian family who had helped me on the Viewpoint.

Dear Trisha,

Just to let you know what happened after the event in case it was hazy for you …

We first heard of you from a woman who came looking for a strong Australian man. She said his wife had a bad arm injury but was still alive. We then started looking for the description that had been given to us of Troy. Later on that same woman, Suzanne, bought you up to us. We could not believe your strength. You probably don't remember the state you were in, but all you kept talking about was finding Troy. At this time you had been badly battered by the wave, your ears were bleeding and full of sand, your body was covered in bleeding cuts and big bruises and your eyes were about to swell shut.

Yet you managed to climb up the lookout in search of Troy, without regard for your personal being.

We were relieved you agreed to stay with us and accept our help. I don't know if you remember much because you were very groggy. Melissa sat with you and tended to your injuries while we went in search of Troy. This was a turning point for our family. We had up to that point been looking out for ourselves, and because we had made the hike up from behind the Viewpoint, we did not realise what had happened on the beach side.

Your injuries bought home the reality to us, and your strength inspired us to stay on and help others. Had we not done that, we would still be full of guilt. For that we thank you.

It meant a lot to me to know that even through the pain and confusion of the tsunami, I had given strength to others.

One of the hardest things this year has been getting past the dates that were special to Troy and me. My birthday on 19 April was a terrible day. The weekend before, Melbourne had played the Saints and I had people over for drinks after the game, which was okay. But then on Tuesday, my actual birthday, Belly, Luke, Carly and Eleanor came over. It was a nice idea of theirs, but I couldn't handle it, and ended up in my room watching a DVD and crying my heart out. In the end they left. Troy had always made my birthday so special and I missed him so much. That night I cried so much I vomited. I had turned twenty-four and my heart was breaking.

Kirsten left for the UK at the end of April to be with her boyfriend, Phil, in Oxford. Just before she went, I asked Reach if we could have a session for some of my close friends including Clint Bizzell. We got into some pretty deep discussions that really helped me work through some of the stuff that had been hanging over my head since the tsunami. I wrote down some of my thoughts during that session.

As I stare at my reflection in the sea, I see the awful truth of what has happened, I see my weak body, no strength, my eyes forced open, my heart aching and my body wanting to give up. The permanent black circles under my eyes, my body uncontrollably shaking. Please turn back the clock, please is someone out there who can help me?

I feel so alone and sorry for myself. I feel unloved, unworthy and unsure.

I am scared of being vulnerable as it hurts too much. To let myself feel all this, it takes over my mind and body. It takes me to a deep dark place. I close my eyes and see the water, I feel the cuts, I hear the screams, I feel fear, I feel peace, I feel Troy.

Four months ago I was proud of who I was. Now all my traits, good and bad, have been put out in front of me and I'm ashamed that I have so much work to do. I am scared that if I let my defences down, all people will feel is my pain and hurt and see my tears. They will get tired of me, just as I am so tired, I am aching all over. I want to talk to people about Troy, but I feel like everyone needs to move on and it's me that's bringing them back.

I need people to understand and accept my way of grieving. I need to embrace how I feel each day. I need to never forget Troy, forget his voice, forget his touch, forget his body, forget his love and forget his care.

Please, Troy, are you out there? I need your help.

In May I took a brief holiday to Europe to visit Kirsten in Oxford, and also Chris Lamb in London. I also caught up with Michelle King, a friend who had just announced her engagement. It was strange to be in London, trying to stay excited for Michelle and talking about her upcoming wedding. One afternoon Michelle and I were at her house in Clapham Common when I was overcome with an urge to move my wedding ring from my left hand to my right. This was a very significant moment for me. That ring had always made me feel safe, and even as I moved it I could feel my insides churn. I was saying to the world that I was no longer a married woman, no longer a wife. I was alone. It hurt to accept that, but somehow I knew that the only way to get over the pain was to go through it, not around it.

Despite everyone's promises and genuine good intentions, I had to face the reality that I alone would get me through my grief. I knew now that there was no magic cure. The pain would always be there, and if I was to cope I needed to learn how to live with it. Happiness was not going to be found in the absence of pain, but rather in the embracing of it. It sounds stupid, but I can't think of another way to put it. Ever since the tsunami, I had been waiting for a moment when things would suddenly be okay again. I was crying out for a time when the thoughts in my head would stop and give me peace. I had tried fighting against them, but that didn't work. I had tried cutting off and ignoring them, but this meant cutting off and ignoring myself. In the end there was no easy answer. I had to walk headlong into the pain and see what was on the other side.

I had gotten into the habit of writing a letter to Troy on the 20th of each month, and I wrote the following from Paris during that trip overseas.

Dear Troy,

Can you hear me? Can you see me lying on this bed with my iPod? Can you hear my sad music? Are you up there, Troy? I feel so terrible, Troy, I am fat and ugly and I want you to be proud of me. I want to be your beautiful wife forever.

Troy, I know you saved my life, did you not know that I did not want to live without you? I can't live without you, you know that. You have made me realise how much you really did love me. You sacrificed your whole life for me. I promise I would have done the same for you. I feel guilty – was I good enough for you? I hate myself when I think that maybe I stressed you out when you were here. I just wanted the best for us.

I get sick of fighting this pain, Troy, but I keep going for you. You are the reason why I can keep going. You know when I said I will love you forever, I meant it. Troy James Broadbridge, my husband, my soul mate, my everything.

I have let everyone down again. I have stuffed up. But you know what, Trisha, you haven't stuffed up, you are just following your instincts. You have finally connected. You are what you are, and you have no one to answer for when you get back.

No one can save you but yourself. Don't be ashamed, Trisha, you had an amazing journey, you did this on your own.

I want to make a difference with the people of Thailand.

I want to start a support group for people that have lost loved ones in a tragic way in every state. Not just for widows but for friends, my friends who are grieving for Troy. Somehow I want to support the people in my life too. It must be hard for everyone. Nothing prepares you for death. Nothing ever could prepare you for this.

I want to be a good friend, I want to be honest. I want to allow people in. I want to give support. I want to share honestly. I want to be okay with who I am. I want to share the goodness I do have somewhere deep down.

Troy, I want your values to live within us.

When I returned from London I threw myself into my work with the Reach Broadbridge Fund and focused on making the education centre in Thailand a reality. Slowly but surely I was taking control of my life rather than allowing myself to stay in that wave forever. A stroke of amazing luck had meant I survived, and now I was using that luck to try and make the world a better place.

I tried to turn painful thoughts of Troy into inspirations to keep working towards building the education centre and taking Reach to South Australia. It was particularly important to me that the centre would be in memory of my husband, under the Broadbridge name. When Troy and I became engaged, I had originally wanted to keep my maiden name, Silvers. But after numerous discussions Troy persuaded me to change my name, as it meant so much to him. I am so glad the centre will carry his name forever.

I also started to see the tsunami on a grand scale, looking at the bigger picture to gain a perspective on my own life by trying to understand how I fitted into this massive event which had no rhyme or reason but just happened. Every time I read a website about the tsunami, I noticed little things like the different death tolls. Often they differed by 10,000 or more. I would look at that number 10,000 and ask myself, 'If Troy had survived, would it be 9,999?' Of course the answer is no. The truth is we deal with death on a grand scale every day. This year alone, close to 15,000,000 people worldwide will starve to death, and it will not rate a mention in the headlines. When I started to think about stuff like that I found it hard to comprehend.

I decided to do the only thing I could do. I began to plan my return trip to Phi Phi Island in September to help build the education centre. And I decided to invite the boys from the Melbourne Football Club to help lay the foundation stone. Perhaps then, once and forever, I would be able to lay my husband to rest.

Chapter 20

End of Season

On 26 July, exactly seven months to the day after the tsunami, I moved out of our Cheltenham home. The decision had been building in me for some time. I had turned Cheltenham into a memorial to Troy – there were pictures of him everywhere and everything about the house reminded me of our times together. A house holds memories in the weirdest places and for a while I needed to hang onto those. I parked our car in the same place. I slept on 'my side' of the bed. Sometimes at the supermarket I would find myself picking something off the shelf that was Troy's favourite, not mine.

The whole routine of my life needed to change if I was going to move forward. I needed to reconnect with friends and establish myself as an independent woman. Making these decisions was far harder than I'd anticipated. For seven months I had been obsessed with being the perfect widow. It was like society casts this role for widows and when you step outside it everyone starts to get uncomfortable. Including me!

Around this time I started to think about whether I could ever form another relationship. When I first returned home having just lost Troy I swore that I would never be with anyone again, that I was Troy Broadbridge's wife and that's who I would be for the rest of my life. But as time has gone on, and after many conversations with my closest friends, I have gradually managed to accept the possibility of a future relationship. I remember talking to Luke Williams and Clint Bizzell about four months after Troy died, and Luke said that he would be pleased for me to be in another relationship because he just wanted me to be happy, and that as long as it made me happy he would support me. Clint agreed with Luke. That was the first time I'd let myself think it might be at all possible. I was surprised at first that the boys thought this way, but that night I realised Troy would have felt the same. Troy and I had even spoken about it once – that if either of us died before the other, all we wanted was for each other to be happy. But we never for a minute thought either of us would die young – we were thinking about twenty years down the track.

That same night with the boys I voiced my fears about whether anyone would ever love me again. I had so much emotional baggage it would not fit on a plane! I felt unattractive, unworthy and unwilling to let anyone close to me. We all laughed about any guy who would take me on – they even said, 'We would give him a medal.' I wondered who would ever want a basket case partner who did not want them to leave the country, leave the state, or even leave the house – and definitely never to go anywhere near water! That fear of losing someone close creeps in all the time.

Moving out of our house led me to think more about the

future, and I've realised that if I was ever to get involved with someone they would have to accept that Troy is and always will be my first love, and that if he were still alive there is no chance I would not be with him. So being with me would mean being with Troy: they could not be jealous of him, and I would not compare them to him. No one will ever replace Troy. What I had with Troy will stay with me forever.

The hardest part for people in my position is that the thing you miss most is the really strong support and security that comes from a loving relationship and yet the very thought of ever trying to find it again fills you with so much guilt, it seems an impossible step to take. I would have judged harshly people in similar situations to mine who re-partnered quite quickly, but now I can see why it happens and how much strength it would take to move on in this way while still maintaining the integrity of the love you lost. I've read that a number of women who lost partners in September 11 have since fallen in love. At first I did not understand how they could, but maybe one day I too will understand. I have to live in the present, not in the past, and not in the future. I need to allow whatever I feel each day to happen, and be true to myself and people around me.

There is no such thing as the perfect widow. Everyone's experience of losing a partner is different. I will not judge others and hope that no one judges me. As long as you follow your instincts and be true to yourself, I think that's the best you can do. That's where I went wrong at the start – I was trying to be someone who was trying to do all the right things and please all the right people and it led me into a downward spiral. I hope that my story helps other women who have lost a partner, because I know now that there is no right way of grieving, nor is there a time limit on the grieving process. So when it came to moving out of Cheltenham, it was like the force of moving towards something was greater than the force of moving away.

Throughout the course of the year, I'd met with a number of tsunami survivors and their families and began to see a real pattern emerge. It put my own grieving in perspective. It seemed there were those who had managed to start the journey forward by being able to see some sense in the future, and then there were those who just could not move forward. It was like they were still trapped in the wave. Sometimes I'd feel myself slipping back there again and I knew how easy that slide could be. A tragedy has a way of defining you which is very hard to break away from. Some people see Troy and by association, me, as the Australian face of the tsunami, but nothing could be further from the truth in terms of how I feel. In a way that trivialises the journeys of those affected by the disaster.

In September, I found out I had been nominated for Young Australian of the Year. It's funny how life plays tricks on you – I had always said I wanted to live an extraordinary life and yet even an honour of this magnitude meant little unless I was feeling happy in myself.

Towards the end of the 2005 season, as my life was changing, Melbourne's finals chances were starting to slip away. Halfway through the year, Melbourne had been one of the premiership favourites, and then with a combination of injuries and poor form, the boys found themselves struggling for a finals birth in the last few games. During the season, I had consciously tried to become less reliant on the footy club for my sense of self and I didn't go to many matches. People come and go in the football world – Troy and I had seen that happen and I knew that I too would need to move on. When I think back to the tribute match and how much a part of the team I felt, I can also see how far I have come. Back then I really depended on that bond and its connection to Troy to give me a reason to keep going. I had needed David Neitz to stand there with his arm protectively around me. All that support was invaluable while I was struggling to find a way forward. But now I don't need the contact as much, knowing that the people who had shared my life with Troy will always be there for me and I've made some great friendships that will last forever. I guess I accept that I now have a different place in the club – I'm not a player's partner anymore but I'm not just a supporter either, because I've seen footy from the inside.

Unfortunately Melbourne's finals campaign was a disaster. Despite their strong finish to the home and away season, and some nail-biting close games, they were thrashed by Geelong in the elimination final. It was not the fairytale end to the season some had predicted at the start of the year but I was fast learning fairytales and perfect endings are few and far between. But I admire that the Melbourne boys did the best they could and did not give up. When you've been behind the scenes at a club you realise how much work they put in, even if it doesn't show on the scoreboard. They should be proud of what they achieved in 2005.

Sandringham made it to the VFL Grand Final, and on Sunday 18 September I was back in the grandstand watching my good friends play for back-to-back premierships. I'd been to heaps of their matches throughout the year. It was strange being part of the crowd because people seemed to recognise me, something I still have trouble adjusting to. The players wore armbands in Troy's honour. Lots of Troy's best mates still played for Sandy so it was really important for those guys to recognise his place in the club's history. I went on to the ground before the game to get an armband – I'd suggested they wear red ones because it was a bit more fun – and wore it for days afterwards.

It was a good match, especially when Sandy was up by 35 points at the 26-minute mark of the third quarter; it was looking like it would be a comfortable win. Then Werribee staged a big last-quarter comeback, getting to within 9 points – what a relief when the siren went! I burst into tears and followed everyone onto the ground, ending up in the rooms watching the boys singing the song. So many of the boys told me they'd played for their mate. The coach, Mark Williams, said after the win that they'd dedicated the match to Troy and wanted to let everyone know they still really missed him. I was in tears, mostly because I was so happy for those boys and felt so much a part of it. The celebrations went well into the night.

Chapter 21

In Troy's Memory

The first public outcome of the Reach Broadbridge Fund was the launch of the fund into South Australia in mid-September. Going there with the Reach crew to train a group of teachers to use the Reach philosophy was the first step in what I hope will be an ongoing presence for us in Troy's home state.

Early in the teacher-training workshop we played a DVD which mapped my personal journey throughout the year, to help explain the power of storytelling in working with kids who had experienced difficulties in their lives. The DVD had a profound effect. It created a sense of connectedness in the workshop which enabled the teachers to open up and share their own stories. Somehow, it became clear to me then that everyone has tragedy in their lives. The stories that emerged from that group of teachers ranged from heartbreaking to uplifting but without exception those stories showed that people, no matter how different their circumstances, are somehow linked by that moment in their lives when they doubt their ability to go on.

Establishing the Broadbridge Education Centre in Thailand was a much more complex process. We were working under pressure the whole time and I kept reminding myself, 'If I can survive a tsunami, I can do this.' Every single thing we needed, from the roof of the building to the nails that would hold it on, had to be shipped over in two massive 40-foot containers. The prefabricated bungalows would all be flat packed. We were really worried about Thai customs and declarations; even though we had contacted all the embassy officials and had advice from shipping companies, no one could confirm how the goods would finally get from the mainland across to Phi Phi Island Village Resort. It seemed every time we solved one problem a new one would arise, yet we were strangely optimistic that somehow it would all happen.

For weeks, donated goods – educational aids, computers, books, art materials, toys – had been arriving at the Reach office. Eventually my family helped me load it all onto the builders' truck that would transport the goods across to the containers, to be shipped mid-August, about six weeks before the building would start. I can still see Dad going up and down the lift of the storage centre with box after box of things for the Thai kids. Their help showed how much my parents had supported me throughout the year. With time, I'd accepted that the two people I had become closest to were the ones I thought would never understand me, and now there are times when I feel like they are the only two people who really do.

The Melbourne players had decided to incorporate the building of the education centre into their end-of-season trip. To raise funds for the boys' expenses, Clint Bizzell and David Neitz organised the Broadbridge Ball in mid-August. It was a very special night – the theme was 'A Touch of Red' in honour of Troy – and it meant a lot to me that they'd decided to come with me to Phi Phi.

There were other pressures as well in the lead up. To find a Thai teacher, we sent out the information to all our contacts in Thailand. Finally we found a woman whose CV seemed to fit and we interviewed her over the phone which was really hard for a person speaking in their second language. But luckily my Thai teacher was there to translate and we gave her the job. I also felt a great responsibility to make the whole thing perfect – I wanted everyone to walk away feeling that they had made a difference and I wanted to give the players an unforgettable experience. It was bigger than planning my wedding but I approached it with the same military-style precision!

An amazing thing happened the week before I left for Phi Phi. The AFL Players' Association donated $250 000 to the Reach Broadbridge Fund! Every year the players make a donation of $15 from their match payments and then that money goes to charities of their choice. In 2005 the players chose to donate another $20 per match in honour of Troy, and the Reach Broadbridge Fund was the lucky recipient. I'd met with the AFLPA five times through the year so I wasn't surprised but the amount was quite a lot more than I thought it would be. Brendan Gale, CEO of AFLPA, and Nathan Buckley presented me and Jim with the cheque on the last *Footy Show* for the year, and an unexpected announcement was made on the night that the Pratt Foundation had donated $50 000 as well. Of course I was overwhelmed by this kind of support – that huge injection of money would enable us to plan things that could really make a difference to young people's lives through programs we could now afford to set up and run.

Jon and a couple of builders went over to Phi Phi two weeks in advance to get the building started, but when they arrived on 15 September everything was held up in customs. Finally, on the night of the Grand Final, Jon rang to say that they'd been able to access the containers. This was the best news I'd had all year, even though it meant that before I'd arrived with the players, the project was running about ten days behind schedule. A big part of me was freaking out, especially when Jon mentioned that there had also been tropical rains holding up the site preparation. Then he told me that the Thai locals had joined in to help with carting the materials from the barge onto the island, and that they were willing to help with the building because they wanted to have it underway before my arrival. Amazing!

The night before we left for Phi Phi I went to Melbourne's Best and Fairest, a great warm-up for the players' end-of-season trip but quite confronting for me, being at that annual event for the first time without Troy. My heart started to break all over again as Paul Gardner spoke dearly of Troy while I was waiting to present an award in my late husband's honour. I was rocked by footage from Round 1, the Tribute Match. Paul Johnson won the inaugural Troy Broadbridge Trophy for the best Melbourne-listed player for Sandringham. And I realised that this trophy – the marking of Troy's contribution to the club, even though he'd only played 40-odd games – was a symbol of the respectful and dignified way the club had handled the loss of a player. It was also another reminder that I needed to give something back to the players by way of thanks for what they had given me.

Forty hours later we were welcomed on to Phi Phi Island, arriving in post-typhoon heat and tropical-strength humidity to find the site looking a bit of a mess at first glance. Earlier in the year I had chosen a beautiful spot for the education centre, behind the Phi Phi Island Village Resort, right next to the little village where locals were slowly returning as the tourist trade began to revive. Behind the site rose the mountains which Troy and I had walked over the day of the tsunami. I loved this location because it was almost like Troy was looking down on it, keeping an eye on proceedings. But the day we arrived there was stuff everywhere.

What pleased me most about the project was the way it bought the whole community together. The Melbourne boys worked flat out for 10 hours a day and the locals chipped in as well. It seemed whenever we needed more supplies, they arrived. The hotel donated a truck for two days and four of the boys went off into the villages to find pavers. Others, from the nearby village, bought water and our confidence grew that we would not only finish the project, but that we were creating something that would stand for generations to come.

At the start it was fair to say a few of the boys were a bit skeptical about the building process. The players had mentioned to me it was important that they work hard to finish the building because, if it was for Troy, a token effort would not be good enough.

The end result was anything but token. It exceeded my expectations ten-fold. Eventually the big moment came, when Jon brought a group of kids from the local school to join the village kids and we officially opened the Broadbridge Education Centre. I will never forget their faces. Or the faces of the players as they looked on at these little kids playing on equipment and reading books in the Centre which had just four days before been non-existent.

Later that afternoon, on Friday 30 September, I took the Melbourne boys on a walk to retrace my final steps with Troy. It was a symbol for me of the incredible emotional journey I had been on and a chance for the players to see for themselves what Troy's final resting place was like.

Despite being evening, it was still hot as we walked across the mountain track to Tonsai. The players were very respectful and I felt proud to be leading them. When we arrived at the beach, I had arranged for a circle of bamboo flares to be lit in exactly the spot where Troy and I had stood when the wave hit. It was sunset and the beautiful Phi Phi waters were calm. We sat, and I expressed my thanks to the players and a few of them shared thoughts of their own.

Darkness began to fall but I had one final journey to make. With the whole team behind me and Belly, Luke and Chris Lamb (who had flown in from London to be with us) at my side, I took a lei of flowers and headed towards to water. The thought of ever setting foot into that water again was petrifying. We walked out together into the sea. Behind me I could feel the support of the players. As my foot hit the water, I felt I was filled again with a new strength. Not one which came from Troy or the players, but one I had found in myself. I walked out to almost waist deep and laid the lei gently on top of the water. I watched it for a second and then turned to go. When I looked up the players were standing in a line behind me. They were linked, with arms around each other. It took me back to the tribute match all those months before, and as I waded towards them, in the very water that had taken my husband, I knew I had the strength to move on.

Chapter 22

The Future

If I have learned one thing this past year it is that nothing in life is certain and no one has the right to judge how a person should, or shouldn't react to tragedy. In my heart I know there is nothing extraordinary about me or anyone else who endures tragedy. In fact it is the ordinariness of all of us that should be the focus. Society's way of moving forward is to make people 'extraordinary', so that they do not have to cope with the reality of knowing that in the darkest moments, when the pain is at its most intense, sometimes all that is left is a person who feels there is no reason to stay alive. There is no flash of light or sudden realisation that life is great and you can cope. There is just the day-to-day struggle, the slow rebuilding process, the love of your friends and that indefinable human quality which enables you to take the next step. I knew I would have to face up to the reality of living a 'normal' life again once the memorial service was over.

Whenever I start to question whether I can go on, I put myself at the centre of my own feelings and I experience a shift. I don't know where it comes from but there it is. It's like I ask myself, can I go on? And I just reply, yes, and it is done. I no longer torture myself with 'what ifs'. Instead I just say, 'it happened'. I accept it, and surprisingly this frees me to start asking the bigger questions. I also know that it was a miracle that I survived the tsunami. I have been given a second chance, and for Troy and for myself I will use this opportunity, I will never sit back or baulk at a risk, I will no longer worry about little things, as I have learnt the hard way that things could be worse.

Sometimes on good days, I think of Troy as an angel. He came to me when I needed him, he pushed me to be a better person. He supported me through my university degree, which I thought I would never get, he allowed me to be true to myself. He set me up financially in the best way that he could, and most importantly he loved me and married me. Then, when he felt I would be okay on my own, he left me. He left me physically and said, 'Trisha, I love you and you know what you have to do now.' I do know, Troy. I will lead an extraordinary existence, I will never settle for second best, and I will never give in. You taught me all I know, Troy, and you were the best teacher in the world. In no way would I want you to be disappointed in me, and in no way would I want to live life disappointed in myself.

This journey has been so long and so hard and I have no idea what life has in store for me from here. All I know is that I have had a second chance, and with that second chance I want to leave others the same legacy Troy left me: a life of hope, a life lived with integrity, passion, determination and love.

How It Happened

At 00:59 GMT on 26 December 2004, a magnitude 9.0 earthquake ripped apart the seafloor off the coast of northwest Sumatra. Over 100 years of accumulated stress was released in the second biggest earthquake in recorded history.

It unleashed a devastating tsunami that travelled thousands of kilometres across the Indian Ocean, taking the lives of nearly 300,000 people in countries as far apart as Indonesia, the Maldives, Sri Lanka and Somalia.

Two hundred and forty kilometres off the coast of Sumatra, deep under the ocean floor, at the boundary between two of the world's tectonic plates, lies a 1200 kilometre trench called the Andaman-Sumatran subduction zone. Very slowly, the lower plate, carrying India, is being forced or subducted beneath the upper plate, dragging down most of South-East Asia and causing huge stresses to build up.

These stresses were released on 26 December. The shaking from this giant mega-thrust earthquake woke people from sleep as far away as Thailand and the Maldives and lasted for eight minutes.

Nobody knows how many people died in the actual quake itself, but scientists have since visited the nearby island of Simueleu and found something astonishing. The whole island has been tilted by the force of the earthquake, causing coral that had been submerged for thousands of year to be thrust out of the water on the east side, and bays in the west to be drained.

Deep under the Indian Ocean, at the epicentre of the quake, the twenty-metre upward thrust of the seafloor set in motion a series of geological events that were to devastate the lives of millions. Billions of tonnes of seawater, forced upward by the movement of the seabed, now flowed away from the fault in a series of giant waves.

The only people in the world to have any idea what had happened were thousands of kilometres away on the island of Hawaii. But, relying on seismic data alone, the scientists at the Pacific Tsunami Warning Center had no idea the earthquake had just unleashed an ocean-wide tsunami. It was a full fifty minutes after they first picked up the tremors before they could issue a warning of a possible local tsunami.

Thirty minutes after the shaking had subsided, the first wave, travelling eastwards, crashed into Sumatra. On the shores directly facing the epicentre, the waves reached heights of twenty metres, stripping vegetation from mountain sides 800 metres inland, capsizing freighters and throwing boats into trees. The city of Banda Aceh, just a few kilometres further round the coast, was almost completely destroyed, losing 200,000 people in just fifteen minutes.

Leaving a devastated Sumatra behind, the series of waves continued across the Andaman Sea towards Thailand.

A herd of elephants in the mountains seemed to know what was coming, as they began behaving strangely, stamping the ground and tugging at their chains, eventually breaking away to run to the hills. Elephants have special bones in their feet that enable them to sense seismic vibrations long before we can.

Due to the complex way in which the seafloor ruptured, some waves set off travelling with the crest first, others travelling trough first. The trough, reaching the shores of Thailand, caused the sea to disappear off the beaches – one of the classic warning signs of an approaching tsunami. Tragically, many tourists went down to the beach to look at fish left flapping on the sand. A few minutes later, the first wave hit Thailand. A thousand tonnes of water crashed down on each metre of beach. At Khao Lak, the wave reached ten metres and caused billions of dollars of damage. The human cost was far greater – nearly 5000 confirmed dead and 3000 still missing.

At the same time, the westbound series of waves were heading for Sri Lanka. In the deeper waters of the Indian Ocean, barely noticeable at just thirty centimetres above the surface, they were travelling at some 800 km/h.

The first wave hit Sri Lanka with no receding sea and no warning. The waves, up to six of them weighing over 100 billion tonnes, rushed inland like a giant tide. As they hit Sri Lanka's southern tip, they began to change direction, an effect called refraction.

The part of the wave closest to the shore slowed down in the shallow water, leaving the outer part, travelling at faster speeds, to bend around the island. The southwest coast of Sri Lanka, the side that should have been safe, was suddenly in the waves' direct line. Cities such as Galle were destroyed; over 4000 people died in this region alone.

The waves carried on further north to India, where they killed 10,000 people.

Next in the waves' line was one of the lowest lying countries on Earth – the Maldives. Miraculously, although eighty people died, the Maldives escaped relatively unscathed. It seems that due to their unique geography – the islands are the tips of underwater volcanoes – and without a continental shelf to push the wave height up, the tsunami just washed through. Coral reefs are also thought to have protected the country, acting like a giant underwater colander, stripping the waves of energy.

As the waves left the Maldives, they passed through a narrow gap between the island chains, focusing their energy directly at Somalia, where 300 people lost their lives.

In Kenya, the waves, when they hit, were small, their energy further removed by the land masses of the Seychelles and Diego Garcia. Authorities in Kenya had also seen the news reports and evacuated the beaches; only one person died – the last victim of a natural disaster that had claimed 300,000 with hundreds still unaccounted for.

Indonesia

Impact: The western tip of the Indonesian island of Sumatra, the closest inhabited area to the epicentre of the earthquake, was devastated by the tsunami. More than 70 per cent of the inhabitants of some coastal villages are reported to have died. The Asian Development Bank says 44 per cent of people in the province of Aceh lost their livelihoods.

Toll: At least 126,000 people died, while at least 37,000 others remain missing. The exact number of victims will probably never be known. The number of homeless is estimated at 800,000.

Aid: At least 160 aid organisations – plus UN agencies – provided emergency food, water and shelter to about 330,000 people, according to the UN Office for the Co-ordination of Humanitarian Affairs (OCHA). The government estimates that reconstruction will cost US$4.5 billion over the next three years. Australia alone pledged a AUD$1 billion aid package. Indonesia has put controls in place in an attempt to prevent dishonest officials siphoning off donations.

Sri Lanka

Impact: Sri Lanka suffered more from the tsunami than anywhere else apart from Indonesia. Southern and eastern coastlines have been ravaged. Homes, crops and fishing boats were destroyed. The International Labour Organisation estimates that at least 400,000 people lost their jobs.

Toll: At least 31,000 people are known to have died, and more than 4,000 are missing. The number of homeless people is put at between 800,000 and one million. In one of the worst single

incidents, at least 1000 people died when a train was struck by the tsunami at Telwatta – the worst train disaster in world history.
Aid: Foreign troops have been helping to clear the wreckage. The government is set to begin rebuilding seaside towns – some from scratch – as part of a US$3.5 billion reconstruction drive. There have been lingering tensions between the government and Tamil Tiger rebels over the distribution of aid.

South-east coast of India
Impact: India's south-east coast, especially the state of Tamil Nadu, was the worst affected area on the Indian mainland. (See below for more details on the Andaman and Nicobar Islands.) In Andra Pradesh state, the World Food Programme estimated some 2000 fishing boats were lost, and the Asian Development Bank estimates India lost some 700km of road.
Toll: More than 8800 people are confirmed dead in mainland India, 8000 of them in Tamil Nadu and almost 600 in Pondicherry (see below for data on the Andaman and Nicobar Islands). Thousands more are still missing. At least 140,000 Indians, mostly from fishing families, are in relief centres.
Aid: Repairing the damage is expected to cost about US$1.2 billion. India has provided aid to other countries hit by the tsunami. Initially it refused outside help itself but later acknowledged that, despite its growing economic and regional strength, it could not cope alone with a disaster on this scale.

Andaman and Nicobar Islands

Impact: Salt water, which washed over the islands, contaminated many sources of fresh water and destroyed large areas of arable land. Most of the islands' jetties have also been destroyed.

Toll: At least 1829 of the islands' 400,000 people are confirmed dead and more than 5500 are missing – 4310 from Katchall island alone.

Aid: India is still refusing international assistance on the Andamans because of the presence of a military base on one island and indigenous tribes on some others. The military has been building extra landing fields on the islands to help with relief. About 12,000 people have been moved to relief camps on larger islands.

Thailand

Impact: The west coast of Thailand was severely hit, including outlying islands and tourist resorts near Phuket. Some bodies may still lie in the rubble of ruined hotels.

Toll: More than 5300 are confirmed dead. More than 1700 foreigners from a total of thirty-six countries are among the dead. Over 2900 are missing.

Aid: Thailand did not ask for disaster relief aid but requested technical help to identify the dead, a huge operation which is still ongoing.

Maldives

Impact: The Maldives consists of 199 inhabited islands, twenty of which have been described as 'totally destroyed'. But the impact on one of the lowest-lying countries on earth could have been much worse. Scientists say the islands may have been protected by their position on the tips of underwater volcanoes: there was no land mass to push the wave height up. The World Bank estimates that international tourist arrivals in the Maldives in January 2005 were down nearly 70 per cent on January 2004 – a major problem for a country where tourism is the main industry.

Toll: At least eighty-two people have died and twenty-six are missing.

Aid: The Asian Development Bank says reconstruction will cost US$304 million, and the government is looking for some US$1.3 billion over the next three to five years. Only a fraction of the money needed has been pledged so far. Recently the government signed a memorandum of understanding with the International Committee of the Red Cross to fund the construction of temporary housing for 9955 people displaced by the disaster. Eighteen of eighty-five temporary units have reportedly been completed.

Malaysia

Impact: Although Malaysia lies close to the epicentre, much of its coastline was spared widespread devastation because it was shielded by Sumatra. However, scores of people were swept from beaches near the northern island of Penang.

Toll: At least sixty-eight people are confirmed dead.

Myanmar (Burma)

Impact: The worst affected area was the Irrawaddy Delta, inhabited by poor subsistence farmers and fishing families.

Toll: Burma's military junta has put the death toll at sixty-one, but the World Food Programme (WFP) says this may be an underestimate. One WFP employee found 200 households where at least one person was missing. Hundreds of Burmese migrants workers living in Thailand are also thought to have died.

Bangladesh

Toll: Two people were reported dead in Bangladesh.

Somalia

Somalia was the worst-hit African state, with damage concentrated in the region of Puntland, on the tip of the Horn of Africa. The water destroyed 1180 homes, smashed 2400 boats and rendered freshwater wells and reservoirs unusable, the UN said in a report early in January.

Toll: Around 300 Somalis are thought to have died, with thousands more homeless and many fishermen still unaccounted for. As many as 30,000 people may have been displaced.

Aid: The UN has called for US$13 million to help tsunami victims. Aid agencies with small ground operations in Puntland have delivered food and relief supplies, as has a German Navy helicopter. Somalia is anarchic and has few roads, presenting aid agencies with a major challenge.

Kenya
Toll: One person drowned in Kenya.

Tanzania
Toll: Ten people were killed in Tanzania.

Seychelles
Toll: One person was killed in the Seychelles.

Source: http://news.bbc.co.uk/1/hi/world/4126019.stm

Acknowledgements

Bridal Party
Chris Lamb, Tracey Silvers, Daniel Bell, Emeli Paulo, Luke Williams, Carly Schmidt, Sam Broadbridge, Kirsten Emes

The Reach Broadbridge Fund
Clint Bizzell, Cameron Bruce, Paige Davies, Katherine Ellis, Emeli Paulo, Carly Schmidt, Luke Williams, and everyone who has contributed time or money, especially:
Kate & Ross Hildebrand and Aarons Outdoors

Melbourne Football Club
including members, staff, players and directors, especially:
Steven Armstrong & Josie Robertson, Matthew Bate, Daniel Bell & Kim Hall, Clint Bizzell & Jennifer Adams, Nathan & Tamara Brown, Cameron Bruce & Julia Pietryk, Nathan Carroll, Aaron Davey & Anna Rowe, Lynden Dunn, Ryan Ferguson, Simon Godfrey & Jacqui Parish, Brad Green & Anna Lodge, Chris Heffernan & Emma Salter, Ben Holland, Cameron Hunter, Mark Jamar, Chris Johnson, Paul Johnson, Travis Johnstone & Jacqui Birt, James McDonald, Brock McLean, Brad Miller, Brent Moloney, Shannon Motlop & Shannon Aranui, David Neitz & Lisa Harry, Michael Newton, Alistair Nicholson & Julia Foley, Phillip Read, Guy & Trudy Rigoni, Jared Rivers, Russell

Robertson & Brooke Aust, Nick Smith, Colin Sylvia, Brendan Van Schaik, Daniel & Melanie Ward, Matthew Warnock, Paul Wheatley & Rebecca Martial, Matthew Whelan & Renee Hawley, Jeff & Stacy White, Luke Williams, Adem & Afijet Yze, Jackie Emmerton, Janette Sutherland, Jo Juler, Chris Fagan, Steve Harris, Neale & Jan Daniher, Paul Gardner, Cameron & Merryl Butler

Sandringham Football Club
including members, staff, players and directors, especially:
Chad Liddell, Rod Crowe, John Mennie, Gerry Ryan

The Reach Foundation
including all crew, staff, directors and sponsors, especially:
Sam Cavanagh, Andrew Cole, Paul Currie, Jodi Deutrom, Kirk Docker, Jeremy Dooley, Dain Fay, Tom Harkin, Jasna Harris, Luke Huysmans, Romi Kaufman, Peter Kaylor, Elise Klein, Sacha Koffman, Hieng Lim, Jules Lund, Tabitha McDougall, Michelle McQuaid, Sue Meehan, Sharon, Sean & Ashlinn Reilly, Tamica Reynolds, Tanj Saraw, Josh Schmidt, Jim, Sam, Mattisse & Tiernan Stynes, Brionhy Sullivan, Andrew Taylor, Mika Tran, Harley Webster, Eleanor Webster

Special thanks to:
Julia Allan & Cade Witnish, Daniel Breese, Wayne, Pam, Sarah, Sam & Jayne Broadbridge, Carers Victoria staff, Raylene Day, Tania Doko, Anna Dusek, Evans family, Brendan & Alex Fevola, Natasha & Anthony Ingerson, Darren & Deanne Jolly, Michelle

King, Ben Lovell, Jesse Martin, Amy Matthews, Lucy McPhail, Luke Molan, Pye family, Liese Roylance, Shaw family, Tom, Kaye, Tim, Tracey & Trent Silvers, Harry & Sally Silvers-Broadbridge, Peter & Tamara Walsh, Leah Williams, Shane & Deanne Woewodin, Kelly Zidziunas

Professional

Robert Jamieson & Margaret Gurry (Blake Dawson Waldron), Michael Albrecht (Albrecht Jewellers), Pippa Grange, Greg Cunningham (Melbourne Physiotherapy Group), Paul Connors (Connors Sports Management), Jon & Catherine Carnegie (Passionfruit Education), Tom Petroro (Flying Start), Jessica Walker (CARE Australia), Mimma Priolo, John Fowler (Le Pine Funeral Services), Staff at Bunurong Memorial Park, Renee Buckingham (RAB Photographics), Silvercircle, Australian Embassy in Bangkok, Department of Foreign Affairs and Trade, AFL, Glenn Archer & Brendan Gale (AFLPA), Staff at Bangkok Nursing Home, Department of Human Services, Bernie Flood & Tim Barrett (Barrett Baxter Bye), Andrew Raphael (AMP), Sue Hines & Andrea McNamara (Allen & Unwin), Dr Andrew Daff

Credits

Quotation on p. v excerpted with permission from *The Invitation* by Oriah Mountain Dreamer (published May 1999). Copyright © 1999 Mountain Dreaming Productions. All rights reserved. May not be reproduced in whole or in part without the permission of HarperCollins Publishers, Inc., 10 E. 53 St., New York NY 10022.

Photo on page 193 is by Jon Carnegie, taken on Phi Phi Island on 30 September 2005.

Illustrated section

Photos of Troy Broadbridge as a young boy and with his family courtesy of the Broadbridge family

Photos of Troy Broadbridge at Sandringham Football Club from author's private collection

Photo of the 2004 Melbourne Football Club team copyright © Elite Sports Properties Holdings Pty Ltd (ESP)

Photos of Troy and Trisha on holiday from author's private collection

Wedding photos by Renee Buckingham, copyright © RAB Photographics, PO Box 455, Diamond Creek 3089, www.rabphotographics.com

Photo of Trisha with David Neitz, Adem Yze and Guy Rigoni by Ryan Pierse, copyright © Getty Images

Photo of Phi Phi Dream and Trisha with Pang Pond from author's private collection

All other photos of Phi Phi Island from unknown sources. Every attempt has been made to find the copyright holders. Where an omission has occurred, the author and publisher will gladly include acknowledgement in any future editions.